# Andrew Taylor

**CAPSTONE**
*be inspired!*

John Wiley & Sons, Inc.

**Other Wiley Editorial Offices**

John Wiley & Sons Inc., 111 River Street, Hoboken, NJ 07030, USA

Jossey-Bass, 989 Market Street, San Francisco, CA 94103-1741, USA

Wiley-VCH Verlag GmbH, Boschstr. 12, D-69469 Weinheim, Germany

John Wiley & Sons Australia Ltd, 42 McDougall Street, Milton, Queensland 4064, Australia

John Wiley & Sons (Asia) Pte Ltd, 2 Clementi Loop #02-01, Jin Xing Distripark, Singapore 129809

John Wiley & Sons Canada Ltd, 22 Worcester Road, Etobicoke, Ontario, Canada M9W 1L1

Wiley also publishes its books in a variety of electronic formats. Some content that appears in print may not be available in electronic books.

A catalogue record for this book is available from the British Library and the Library of Congress.

ISBN 13: 978-1-4112-776-7

Typeset by 11/16 pt Swiss721LtBt by Thomson Digital
Printed and Bound in Great Britain by TJ International Ltd, Padtow, Cornwall, UK

Substantial discounts on bulk quantities of Capstone Books are available to corporations, professional associations and other organizations. For details telephone John Wiley & Sons on (+44) 1243-770441, fax (+44) 1243 770571 or email corporatedevelopment@wiley.co.uk

# Dedication

As ever, for Sam, Abi, and Bec ... and this time,
Lucy, Sophie, and Tom

# Contents

# Acknowledgements

This book was born out of the *Aftershock* column in the *Sunday Times*, and it is to the readers of the column that I owe the first debt of gratitude. Most of what I know about redundancy, how people react to it, how people cope with it, and how they turn it to their advantage, I learned from the hundreds of letters and emails which they have sent me.

At the *Sunday Times*, Martin Ivens, Karen Robinson, and Sian Griffiths have all played important roles at different times in translating the ideas in my head into the column in the paper. I've had professional help, too, from my agent, Mandy Little, and from John Moseley and Jenny Ng at Capstone. Between them all, they have saved me from more mistakes and embarrassments than I care to remember, and I am much more grateful to them than I have ever admitted.

I've also had a lot of help and advice from personal friends who have shared their thoughts and experiences with me. I can't hope to list them all, but among those who may recognise their stories are Julian Bene, Bob Barton, Chris Collin, Richard and Diana Organ, Michael Phillips, Alison Roberts, Jean Roberts, and Richard Taylor.

I refer several times in the book to the huge value of having an understanding partner. Living with someone who is going through redundancy is hard; living with someone who is writing a book about it is probably even harder; and living with me is maybe hardest of all. I've been more than fortunate to have Penny at my side right from the start, first as my soon-to-be-wife and then as my just-become-wife. Somewhere in the book, I refer to her as 'saintly', which, I'm glad to say, may not be a description she or many other people would recognise at once – but when I look back over the past two or three years, it doesn't seem too much of an exaggeration.

I also say in the book that in getting through redundancy, illness, and other crises, you need to be lucky. That's certainly true, but dealing with illness also requires the care and dedication of a skilful doctor and medical team – and in Dr Tim Littlewood and his NHS colleagues at Oxford's John Radcliffe Hospital, I have had those in spades. Grateful doesn't begin to express how I feel.

Andrew Taylor, Knowl Hill, January 2008

# Introduction

A couple of years ago, I was made redundant – shoved off the treadmill of a job I had been doing for more than ten years, and left floundering around in the employment market.

Like everyone else in the same position, I was angry, frightened, and anxious, often all at the same time. I made up bloodcurdling schemes of how I might get my own back, and I worried that, at 53, I would never work again. I wondered how I would afford to pay for my children going through university, and I spent long hours working out whether the few bits and pieces of pension I had built up over the years would pay for my old age. I asked myself again and again whether it was all my fault, although no-one had ever complained about the way I did my job. For a time, it felt very lonely – but I wasn't alone. Thousands of people in their late forties or early fifties go through the same experience, as I found when I started to write a newspaper column about it. The column, in the *Sunday Times*, was called *Aftershock*, and that – the aftershock of redundancy – was what it was about.

Sometimes, as in my case, it's a sudden, brutal push in the back; sometimes it follows months of anxiety as a company downsizes and reorganises. It may be accompanied by a suitcase full of money, share options, and pension rights, or the deal may be the absolute minimum that the law allows. It may be camouflaged as early retirement, or it may be a humiliating vote of no confidence by an employer. However it is dressed up, redundancy is the modern Black Death of the middle-aged. As they turn 50 and start to think about their pensions, something like a third of the working population find themselves out of a job; five years later, at 55, that figure has gone up to 50 per cent.

And for every one who is actually pushed out, hundreds more worry that they might be. Redundancy hangs over their lives like a dark cloud: people who never dreamed they would lose their jobs find themselves with a 50/50 chance of being on the scrap heap at the very time they ought to be using the experience they have amassed over a lifetime, and building up a few savings for themselves – the time that should be the most rewarding of their working lives. It is a terrifying prospect, but an increasingly common one.

But there is a silent army of the discontented as well who, whether their jobs are secure or not, travel dully into work each day wondering why they are doing so, and dreaming wistfully of a more exciting, more fulfilling life. 'One day,' they say, 'I'll jack it all in and buy a smallholding. Or travel. Or start my own business. Or become a teacher.' One day. But they never do.

## DISASTER OR OPPORTUNITY?

It was when that thought struck me that I began to see that what had felt like a disaster was really an opportunity: the treadmill I had been pushed off was just that – a job that I was doing for no better reason than that I had done it the day before, and that it paid the bills. I realised with something of a shock that I hadn't been particularly proud of the work that I did for some time; I had stopped looking forward to going into the office without ever realising that it was happening. And over the following months, as more and more people wrote to the *Aftershock* column and told me that redundancy had been the best thing that could have happened to them, I gradually realised how *big* an opportunity it was.

Today, three years on, I know exactly what their stories meant. Like many of the people who wrote to me, I'm earning less and living more: if I could rewind my life and have it all over again, I certainly wouldn't miss the experience of being thrown on my own resources. I'm living the life I want to, and not the one I used to think I had to. This book is the story of how I got there, and a rough-and-ready road map for other people on the same journey.

## TAKING CONTROL

It's all about taking control of your life.

Imagine you are standing on a rocky ledge above the sea – high enough to be uncomfortable, but certainly not dangerous. Beneath you, people are splashing about in the water – shrieking with the cold, perhaps, but swimming, diving, and having a wonderful time. You've seen them jump in from the exact same spot where you are standing and shivering, and all you have to do is follow them. But you don't.

A few brave souls make the jump at once, of course; they would take one sniff of the free, fresh sea air, clench their fists, and leap off the rock without a second thought to join in the excitement. Well, this book isn't for them. Most of us pause, some only for a few moments and some until they are shivering and miserable with cold. Some hang around unhappily on the ledge and never jump at all. Some need a push to get off that chilly rock and into the sea to have fun. I was one of those.

## MY STORY

It's not a question of who or what is responsible, and it doesn't have to be redundancy; as we'll see in the course of this book, all sorts of shocks and setbacks can send your life off in a different direction. It might be a serious illness, which is nobody's fault, or a divorce, which may well be your own – and my train has stopped at both those stations too – but the important thing is to get into that water and start splashing around. And redundancy is a good place to start. When you're ill, after all, the only person to shout and swear at is God who, even if you happen to believe in him, seems annoyingly impervious to your anger: when a relationship breaks up, you may go for the other person in a fury, but you're likely to find that will simply complicate the whole messy business. But at least when you're made redundant, you can always be bitter about the company – it may not be God, but it is big enough not to be hurt too much. Anyway, this was my story . . .

I was comfortable enough at work, if not particularly happy. After all, I'd done the same thing every morning for months – years, probably, if I ever stopped to think about it, which I didn't. Off the train, a 20-minute walk through London to Mayfair, let myself into the building in the corner, next to the art gallery, climb the three flights to the office where I worked, and congratulate myself briefly with a middle-aged sort of smug, self-deceiving satisfaction on having had a decent amount of exercise for the day.

On that particular morning, my colleague Christine was already sitting in her room, as she usually was, next to the fax machine that brought in most of the orders from the Middle East television company we both worked for. I barely glanced in as I called out over my shoulder, 'Fancy a coffee?' No reply – but then, if she was on the phone, there often wasn't. First thing in the morning for us was lunchtime in Dubai, and she might well be locked into a call with one or other of our various bosses.

I'd worked as a journalist in the Gulf for five years before I came back to London, and after that, during the eleven years I had been working in Dubai Television's London office, I'd stayed in close touch with a lot of the people there. My bosses, by and large, had become my friends, which is just the way that Arabs often like to do business. I sat down to turn on my computer, check the newswires, and look through my emails. I would call the Dubai office in a moment to discuss how we would handle the day's news, and no doubt we would have a bit of a chat – tease each other about how hard we did or didn't work. Depending on whether we were in Dubai or in London, we might complain about how hot or how cold it was, and we'd ask about each other's families. Just another day, really. But first, I would get a coffee for me and Christine.

Before I could get up, though, she came into the office – slowly, her head down so that her face was hidden by her long, blonde hair. I was concentrating on the computer screen, and she just stood silently by my desk for a moment; and when I did look up, I could see that she was close to tears. 'Oh, Andrew, I don't know what to say,' she said, and I knew that something was horribly wrong. A close friend was seriously ill. Someone had died. She'd had a huge row with her husband. Whatever it was, I wanted to stand up and give her a hug: 'Christine, what's the matter?' I said. She looked almost painfully hurt and vulnerable.

She just held out the scrap of paper that was in her hand. 'I can't tell you. Just read this,' she said. So I did. It had the Dubai Television letterhead, so it was clearly about someone we knew in Dubai; it was in English, not Arabic, so it was meant for us to read, not simply to pass on elsewhere. It was only a day or so before that they had been telling me how pleased they were with the work of the London office; no doubt this was going to be a vaguely embarrassing but very enjoyable email telling us all how clever we were.

But why was Christine so upset about it? 'To Mr Andrew.' They often did that – the odd mixture that I had come to love of formal Mr and friendly first name. 'This is to inform you that from May 31$^{st}$, your contract will not be renewed. You should contact the Personnel Department to arrange payment of your three months' pay in lieu of notice.'

All of a sudden, I was there, in the water. Just when I thought they were patting me on the back, they were shoving me over the edge.

## FIRST FEELINGS

My first feelings, predictably enough, were a mixture of anger and fear. I was angry that they had pushed me, these people I had taken for my friends, and I felt fear because I didn't know how deep or how treacherous these waters that I was suddenly floundering about in might prove to be. It didn't take long, even for someone as close to functional innumeracy as I was, to add up my monthly outgoings and see that with zero monthly income, the future might not be that bright. But even then, fluttering around almost unnoticed at the back of my mind, was another feeling trying to get out. There was an unmistakeable sense of freedom and exhilaration – maybe I wasn't going to have a salary for some time, but unless I was very careless in finding whatever it was that I would do next, I wouldn't be getting on that hated morning train either.

With hindsight, the anger and fear were exaggerated. After all, the people who had fired me were my bosses, and anyone who thinks of his employers as his friends is making the same mistake as a lion tamer who imagines he gets on pretty well with the lions. They may nuzzle up against you for a while (the lions, not the bosses, I mean) but you'd better believe that if it suits them, they'll tear you to pieces and never notice that you've gone. There's not much point in being angry with a big cat who doesn't know any better. And to be honest, if someone offered you a better job somewhere else, you wouldn't let the fact that you got on well with the boss stand in your way. Sauce, goose, and gander come to mind.

As for the fear – well, very few things turn out to be as dreadful as you think they might. I had a soon-to-be-wife who – with a bit of luck – wouldn't let me starve; if I had to, I could dig holes in the road for a while, or hold up an advertising board in the street. My income wasn't actually going to be zero. And anyway, wasn't this what banks were for?

So, as the weeks passed, those feelings grew less and less. But the feeling of exhilaration, that tiny bird that had fluttered around almost unnoticed at the back of my mind – that grew, day by day, until it soared like an albatross. At 53, when most people I knew were winding down towards their pensions, I was free. I might be more or less on my uppers, and wondering what my next step should be – but it was all up to me and nobody else. There was no limit to what I could do.

# Chapter One

## Thrown Off the Treadmill

**C**hristine was the exception.

When you get a four-line fax ending sixteen years with the same employer, you start to find out what sort of friends you have. In my case, cerebral, caring, and sensitive: one asked straight out whether I'd been caught with my hands in the till or climbing into bed with the boss's wife; while another, equally supportive, pointed out that I hadn't actually been made redundant. I'd been that for at least 30 years, he explained. It was just that somebody had finally noticed.

A few years before, I'd had a frightening seven-week stay in a cancer ward, which does a pretty radical job of reassessing priorities. Then, there was little I could do but hope for the best – but at least this time, I could set about finding myself a new job. I left a message on one friend's telephone, thinking he might help me find a bit of freelance work as a journalist to tide me over. I'd had a bit of bad news, I said: could he give me a call? When he did call me back, and when I explained what had happened, rather than sympathy, I got anger.

'I thought you were going to tell me that the cancer had come back when I got your message,' he said. 'I reckoned you were going to tell me that you were going to die. And now you say you've just lost a crappy job which you didn't like much anyway!'

But in fact, I didn't want sympathy. Jokes had always worked better for me – whatever the disaster, there are limits to how much help friends can be. When I phoned my friends after I was diagnosed with cancer, every single one of them, once they'd said how sorry they were, asked the same thing: 'What can I do?' Generally the answer is 'Not a lot.' Your first thought is usually that you have to sort these things out for yourself – although that time, one very good mate called BJ did find himself with a role. After I'd done the shaking-the-fist-at-God bit, I told him that I had cancer – and he had a shock when he heard how he could help me. Several years before, I'd lent another mutual friend a few hundred pounds when he was in a crisis, and he had run off without paying me back. I've never seen him from that day to this. 'I'll tell you what you can do,' I said to BJ. 'If I die, you can get my money back for me. You can do what you like with it – give it to charity, throw a party, or buy yourself a smart new suit, but I want my money. I don't want that guy thinking that he's won.'

In the scheme of things, worrying about a long-gone bad debt when you're faced with the possibility that you might not see Christmas seems mad, and perhaps it's significant that we were both born in Yorkshire – but he understood exactly how I was thinking. 'You've got it' he said, very calmly, and he would have done it too – except that I didn't die, and he did, not long afterwards. Perhaps I was wrong about God being impervious to your angry attacks. And who said he doesn't have a rather black sense of humour?

This time around, though, at first glance there didn't seem to be anything to ask my friends to do – although, as we'll see, I reconsidered that conclusion quite quickly. But what was there to be sympathetic about? I had been fairly disenchanted with my job for at least a couple of years, and I had been doing exactly what I'd always promised myself I would never do – coming into work each day just because

I'd gone in the day before, and because it paid the mortgage. And in the past, when I had been safely on the 'smug salaried worker' side of the fence, the grass on the redundancy payment side had always seemed particularly lush and green; I had always thought there was a fairly convincing divide between people who had seen large helpings of redundancy money dolloped on their plates and paid off their mortgages with it, and those who hadn't been so lucky. Some had even, Oliver Twist-like, held up their plates for seconds – one friend had been made quite profitably redundant by her employer and then, when the accountants had done their sums again or the management had changed their priorities, she'd been reappointed. And not long ago, she'd been made redundant – even more profitably – for the second time, by the same employer. Far from being a disaster, my fax message might just prove to be my ticket for the gravy train that I had thought I would never board at all. I licked my lips in slavering anticipation of the feast to come.

## GOING TO THE LAWYERS

For a day or so, every paper I picked up seemed to be full of nothing but stories of huge payouts for city bankers, stockbrokers, and football managers. Rows of 0's and £ signs swam around in my head as I dreamed lazily of stuffing my snout into this welcoming trough. Perhaps my biggest problem would be to decide whether to have leather seats in the Porsche that my employers – my ex-employers – were clearly going to have to pay for. In fact, making them pay would give me a huge amount of pleasure, quite apart from the fun of driving the Porsche. So I found myself a lawyer – which wasn't a fashion accessory I had ever dreamed of buying. I told myself that I could be the Victoria Beckham of litigants, and played with the idea of getting someone really expensive just because I could – after all, I mused, it was a good investment, and the huge redundancy cheque that the courts were going to award me would cover the cost anyway – but some faint stirring of intelligence stopped me, and I rang another old mate instead.

He was a solicitor who specialised in employment law, so he would obviously be able to help. I could almost smell the swill in the trough I was about to start gulping down. Wrong.

'Look,' he said, sounding faintly embarrassed, in the way that only lawyers can, 'we generally represent the companies, not the individuals. We'd be more likely to be appearing against you rather than for you.' It seemed a bit harsh, but I could see the point. Companies tend to have more money than the people they sack, and lawyers are traditionally fond of money. But, being a mate as well as a lawyer, he had a better idea. 'There is one guy who we always hate to have coming up against us. I'll give you *his* name,' he said.

And that moment marked the dawning of reality. I never actually met the lawyer he'd recommended face to face; instead, we had a series of telephone conversations for which – bless him – he charged me just half an hour of his time. I was not, after all, Victoria Beckham but Victor Meldrew. Now, I know lots of jokes about lawyers, but this one was offering wisdom over the phone at a knockdown rate: there is no pot of gold, he said. The trough is empty. No-one is going to give you sackloads of used £50 notes. No leather seats, no Porsche, not even a push-bike. If I wanted to, he said, I could sue the company I had worked for, and I might get an extra month's pay out of them – but even if I won, it would probably cost me more than that to get it. Given the spectrum between the £12 million settlements I'd been reading about and a flea in the ear, he reckoned that my case fell decidedly closer to the flea in the ear. I was on my own, with a lot more free time than I'd planned for. It was time to take a more realistic look at the pool I was now swimming in.

**SO WHAT HAD OTHER PEOPLE DONE?**

I'd heard lots of stories about friends who had suddenly found themselves without a job. One of them, Michael, had run a very successful stationery business for 30 years until it went bust. Now, he and his wife were living on a narrowboat, and happier than they had ever been in their lives, he told me. 'There was an amazing feeling of liberation when it actually happened,' he said. 'For years, I'd been juggling with the figures, trying to work out ways not to go bankrupt – and when the day came that there was no more juggling to be done, I simply felt relieved. In an odd sort of way, it was like being set free.'

But for every one like me and Michael, there were dozens, maybe hundreds, more who simply walked away from jobs they had fallen out of love with. A vicar I had known in the north of England had shocked his parish during one Sunday morning service by announcing that he was leaving the ministry to go and drive a steam train. He wasn't leaving the church, he said, and he hadn't lost his faith – but he did think he could get more out of life by doing something he had always dreamed of. A successful journalist had turned his back on the BBC at the age of 50, and was delivering groceries for Tesco. 'It had never occurred to me before, but for 20 years or more, I had been knocking on doors knowing that the people inside just wanted me to go away. Often they told me so, in no uncertain terms – but now I turn up with their shopping, and they're really glad to see me,' he said. David Cornthwaite, who hated his job as a graphic designer, maybe went a bit far by throwing it all up and setting off to skateboard across Australia. By the time he had completed the 3600-mile journey, he had gone through more than a dozen tubes of sunscreen and thirteen pairs of shoes; he had blisters on his feet, and a grotesquely over-developed right calf muscle caused by pushing his skateboard along – but his first thought was to plan another long-distance journey. 'I'm not going back to the day job,' he said. Well, you're allowed to do crazy things at the age of 27.

Back in the real world where the rest of us live, another friend of my own, Rick, had lost his job after a successful career in business. He had done well at the company, and he had no reason to suspect that he wouldn't stay there until it was time to draw his pension. It certainly wasn't his fault that the whole business was restructured, and that there was suddenly no place for him. Over the following six months, he put together a portfolio career in which he worked as a part-time director for a couple of companies and did regular charity work. He wasn't earning as much as he had done before, but he wasn't spending anything like as much time on the road or away from home either. To anyone on the outside, it looked as if he had made some pretty shrewd choices to get where he wanted to be.

'It may look like that, but I would never have done any of it if I hadn't been made redundant,' he says now. 'In a way, it's pretty shaming to admit that. I'm not stupid: I can work out what's going to make me happy, and now I think I've just about done that. But I wouldn't have made those choices on my own. I would still have been a wage slave, just doing what I did because I was paid for it, and making myself miserable.'

Perhaps in my old life, justifying to myself the fact that I was still going into the same old job and hadn't made any of those life-changing choices, I would have allowed myself a private sneer about all this upbeat optimism, and a few condescending words about how well they were all doing at finding an EPNS lining to a very black thunder-cloud. But that was my old life: now even I could see that it wasn't like that. All these people really *were* happier than they had been before. My double-edged, condescending words of commendation should have been aimed not at them, but at all the people who were stuck doing the unfulfilling jobs they had been doing for years. If it wasn't enthusing them, filling them with a sense of achievement and exciting them each Monday morning, they were the ones who were, quite literally, making the best of a bad job.

## THE LUCKY GENERATION?

For my generation, more than anyone before us, it doesn't have to be like that. Apart from all the people of my sort of age who suddenly find they haven't got a job any more, there are probably millions who walk into work on a Monday morning and think bleakly, 'Why am I doing this?' There are all sorts of reasons why they are, of course, and the bank manager could point out a few of them quite quickly – but the point is that there are choices to be made.

The economists, accountants, and management consultants – people I once had to listen to – put it with characteristic lucidity when they talk about a 'backward sloping supply curve of labour'. Just thinking about that self-regarding gobbledegook and realising that I may never have to pretend to understand it again or smile in agreement at the suits who spout it was like a draught of pure oxygen. What it means – I think – is that if you pay people too much, they stop working sooner. Because of the mad way the economy and house prices have worked over the last few decades, increasing numbers of people can think about setting out to paddle their own canoes long before the 65 years that our fathers sweated towards.

Past generations didn't earn so much so quickly, and had more of it tied up in the untouchable pensions that my friends and I can only dream about. We may not have the untouchable pensions – in fact, more and more of us are going to have to keep on earning money one way or another for a lot longer than we expected – but, right now, we have a choice that they didn't have. Of course, it may all go wrong, and a lot of us may wake up later to find out that we weren't as secure as we thought we were – but then, we all know what J.M. Keynes cheerily said everybody was in the long run: Dead, and for a long time too.

And so it slowly dawned on me that perhaps there actually *was* a positive side to my predicament. Maybe, I thought, I might just wait a few months before I started to search for the opportunity to grovel before some pompous seat-polisher in charge of car-park tickets in some soulless office building on the A40. Maybe I might stop hating Monday mornings. The next time I put a suit on, I thought with a frisson of guilty satisfaction, might just be some way off – or maybe, just maybe, I might never even think of wearing one again.

**BURN THE SUIT!**

And that was the Eureka moment when I thought of the television advertisement. At 18, said the commentary, over pictures of a fresh-faced and eager young boy whose tie was a bit too big for his neck, you bought your first suit; at 35, it went on, with a confident alpha-male swaggering across the screen and sweating pure testosterone like a mating baboon, it was time for your first bespoke suit.

(I could just about remember that hideous pas-de-deux with some simpering ninny stroking his hand up my inner thigh. 'Suits you, sir.' 'Which side do you dress, sir?' 'Will that be three buttons on the cuff or four, sir?') And then at 50 – if, of course, you had been saving with whatever bank or building society it was that was paying for the advert – you burned the thing.

That was pure ad-speak, of course; it wasn't that simple. The advertisement, I seemed to remember, showed a naked, suit-less figure celebrating his new-found freedom with a Tarzan-style leap into a clear mountain pool, which frankly didn't seem such a good idea, and probably didn't represent anything like reality anyway. I wasn't in quite that position. And anyway, if he was that confident about the future, then the fat, smug prig of my imagination must have been saving all his life for his old age, just like his mum had told him to. He was, I thought, Johnny No-Mates, not Johnny Weissmuller.

I certainly wasn't confident enough in the future at that early stage to go rampaging naked through the jungle, and in any case, I hadn't actually decided to set the suit on fire – I'd had it ripped off my back, rather suddenly and unexpectedly, and set alight without my having had much to do with it. And somehow, tomorrow had always seemed a better day to start saving than today. Although I had built up all the usual middle-class bits and pieces of a mortgage and a few scraps of pension along the way, I had no big pot of savings to draw on. Since my lawyer friend hadn't been able to work any magic, my late lamented employers didn't seem likely to help out in that regard – and I had two children at university and another one about to go there. And my age didn't help: I'd joked rather sadly for a while that I was at that awkward age – too old to be a toy-boy, and too young to be a sugar-daddy – but now the joke had turned round to bite me. At 52, according to everything I read, I was too old for another job, and too young for a pension.

But the same principle applied. I could burn the wretched suit instead of trying to find another office to wear it in. People had been telling me that it could take a few months to find a new job – but with a bit of clever footwork, a few months could be made to last for ever. One way or another, I would have to make some money, but it certainly didn't need to be as much as before. And it could be fun. I really did have the chance to have fun. Perhaps, I dreamed, it was time to buy a narrowboat and turn into a canal bum. Or learn Arabic. Or start growing chrysanthemums. Or turn myself into an artist, like another old friend I knew. (Even I found that one a bit ambitious!) Maybe I could become a poet, or learn to play the saxophone, or ride a motorbike. Perhaps redundancy was just Fate's way of giving me the great big kick up the backside that I had needed, and telling me to do something with my life.

The message behind that kick was clear: Burn that suit you've always hated wearing! Drop the season ticket in the bin, see how many pieces you can break your umbrella into, and flick two fingers at corporate Britain. What was it I had wanted to do before I got sucked into that mind-numbing commute? Now could be just the time to do it.

## NOTES

- The anger, the fear, and the anxiety are all natural. But so is the optimism that sees redundancy as an opportunity. There are other worlds out there.
- Forget the mega-pay-off. If it happens, it's great — but the chances are, it won't.
- We all have friends who have been made redundant — how have their lives changed, and what can those changes suggest to you?

# Chapter Two

## What Am I Going to Do?

**S**o what on earth am I going to do? Over the next few days, that question kept coming back into my head. I wrote letters and emails, I made phone calls, I drew up complicated schedules of job-seeking activities that reminded me of the revision plans I'd produced as a child. (They served much the same purpose, incidentally, keeping me from doing any actual job-seeking in the same way that sketching out the revision plans had been a substitute for wrestling with French irregular verbs.)

What am I going to do? It would hit me in the middle of a meal, or as I watched television. I would wake up in the small hours, thinking excitedly that I had found a solution, and then realising that it was all a vague but very powerful dream. With hindsight, all the things I *was* doing were useful, but only in the sense that they were keeping me busy. The real achievement of those early days was in working out how to cope with the shock of losing my job.

## ARE THERE ANY RULES?

I guess I was still at the shaking-your-fist stage. In fact, after the first few days, it wasn't at my employers – I had more or less stopped thinking about them once I had realised that there was no chance of getting any more money out of them – but at the whole situation. But I also wanted to understand what was happening to me. On one level, of course, it was simple enough – the company I worked for didn't need me any more, so they had got rid of me. End of story.

But I wasn't the first person to go through this experience. How had other people dealt with it? Were there any rules, any general guidelines, to how people felt? I have never had a great deal of time for academics who use long words to describe short ideas, and hide what they mean behind the way that they say it – but I thought that a look at the studies that had been done on coping with problems like redundancy might help to put the way I was feeling into some kind of context.

One of the things a counsellor will tell you is that there are five distinct stages to a sense of loss. (If you are old enough to remember the Fry's Five Boys milk chocolate bars, which showed five separate pictures of boys' faces as they passed through the stages of desperation, pacification, expectation, and acclamation before they got to 'Realisation – it's Fry's!' then you will find this bit hard to take seriously. Perhaps that's where the academics got the idea.) Those five stages of the advertisement of my childhood are replicated in the textbooks by denial, anger, bargaining, depression, and acceptance – and they apply pretty well to dealing with losing your job, or with getting sick or seeing your relationship break up into a million pieces, come to that. There are particular phrases that come into your head:

'It must be some mistake . . . '
'How dare they . . . ?'

'But if I . . . '
'Not again!'
'Oh well . . . '

The 'bargaining' phase can be particularly tricky: if you're arguing with the people who have sacked you, it won't work, and if you're arguing with yourself, it will just hurry you through to the depression stage, which is where you want to spend as little time as possible. When I was sick, I started trying to propose deals with God, even though I'd never believed in him or taken him particularly seriously. 'If I can only live to see my children grow up . . . ' I would propose, as the basis of a bargain which would lead me to accepting the idea of having cancer. Now that they are grown up, incidentally, and I seem to be better, I can only hope that if he does exist, then he wasn't listening.

All those different stages were beginning to sound quite familiar to me: I could think of times already when I had felt each one. But with the benefit of hindsight, I can see now that I went through the series of emotions not once but dozens of times, and in a more or less random order. I might get the whole gamut in a period of 20 minutes; I might miss out on one or other of them for days or weeks at a time, and then come back to drink my fill of anger, denial, or whatever a bit later on. You can't predict which of them you're going to go through at any particular time, but you can guarantee that, one way or another, you will go through the lot.

**GIVE ME BACK MY JOB!**

So how do people express these different emotions? That's how they *feel*, but what do they *do*? The answer to that one, of course, is that there are as many ways of reacting as there are different people, and that the way that suits one person won't suit another – but there are a few generalisations that seem to apply to most of the people I met and spoke to.

The first thought for many of us is that whatever it is that's been taken from us – our job, our health, a stable and settled relationship, or anything else – we want it back. That's where the initial anger and fear I had felt when I was thrown off the treadmill had come from – anger at having something snatched away, and fear that I wasn't going to be able to replace it. But as the anger and fear die down, many people are surprised and probably rather hurt to find that they have actually been thrown off the treadmill at all. After all, they have been happily scampering around like well-fed hamsters for as long as they can remember – and all they want now is to clamber back as quickly as possible onto another treadmill which will be as similar to the one they left behind as they can possibly make it.

All this, of course, applies to women just as much as to men, although my own entirely unscientific observation is that generally, women seem to get over the first shock much more quickly than men. Once they have accepted that the disaster they may have been worrying about for months has actually happened, they are more likely to start looking around in different places for a new way to fill their lives. They may want another treadmill, but they are far more likely to want a different one, one that works at a different speed and has probably been set up in a different cage. Depending on where you are standing, you can say they are more adaptable or less determined than men – but they are certainly less likely to settle for more of what they have left behind.

There is always an unspoken suspicion that perhaps we were probably to blame for being thrown off the treadmill in the first place. Although we may have been on it for years, we may not have been scampering fast enough, or perhaps our scampering skills were a bit out-of-date and rusty. We probably won't admit this to anyone else, but deep down inside, many of us – even most of us – may well be wondering whether we were ever really worthy of our place on the treadmill at all. That thought is too dreadful to bear, and the most obvious way we can see to keep it at bay is to find ourselves another wheel to run in. If we've been made redundant, we will draw up long lists of potential employers, polish our CVs, and possibly bone up on our IT skills; if it's a relationship that's falling apart, we may wonder sadly where we went wrong – but, to continue the hamster metaphor for a moment, we will never ever let our gaze stray beyond that vision of another happy cage, with fresh food and sawdust, and the wheel rattling happily round and round again. That, we think with passion, a bit like Mole in *Wind in the Willows*, is *home*. (This is my metaphor, and I'll mix it as often as I like, thank you.)

## BREAKING FREE?

From that perspective, the place where the treadmill was set up may seem like a warm and cosy nest – but there may also be a feeling that the cage represents a history of imprisonment. Like me as I sat on all those morning trains, my mind in neutral and my eyes gazing sightlessly at the newspaper, we may not have realised for years that we were locked up at all. The prison bars can be made in all sorts of ways, so a safe, secure, unchallenging job is just one of many types of cage. Some people get locked into a relationship; for others, bizarrely, years of good health can have much the same effect. What's never risked is never rated. Recovering from serious illness, with its stark revelation that everything is fragile, and may suddenly shatter in pieces, may give our life a new edge and urgency we had never dreamed of before.

Think of the cage like that, and we may step out of it, shake our heads in surprise for a moment, and then walk confidently away with scarcely a backward glance. We may, if you like, come to an accommodation with the situation: this is how it's going to be, so this is how I am going to turn it to my advantage. I guess it's a sort of bargaining, like the theorists say. There are certainly people who respond to redundancy like that – they leap with relish into the new world of self-employment, franchises and business start-ups. If it's the break-up of a relationship that has suddenly given them their liberty, they will be the ones joining new societies, following up old contacts and making new friends; and if it's the recovery from illness, they may offer their own private thanks for their good fortune by turning their old lives inside out in some way, setting off on a long trip to India, perhaps, sailing around the world, or going to live in a croft in the outer Hebrides.

Is that a better response? There's no better or worse, but it's certainly a different one. For some people it works well, even if the confidence that these people show the world may be more imagined than real. The point is that the confidence *seems* to be there; they cope with the shock of the world outside by putting up a show of bravado. That's not to be undervalued; I have a sneaky feeling, supported by no evidence at all, that most courage comes from somewhere like that.

## SHOWING WHAT YOU CAN DO

But courage on its own isn't enough – after all, when you tell most people that they are being very brave about something, they panic inside and wonder what it is that they have misunderstood about the situation. Most of us need to be able to show people what we can do. When we're young, such showing off is usually fairly simple – wanting to run faster than anyone else, for instance, or get better marks, or show that you care less about whatever marks you get. It may be wanting to drink more than the man standing next to you at the bar, or drive your car faster than the next man at the traffic lights (and neither of these, incidentally, is an exclusively male preserve) but supposing that you survive all those challenges with both your licence and your life, by the time you reach middle age, you're probably a bit more subtle about the way you set out your stall.

That doesn't apply to everyone, of course. We've all met and loathed the 'I've got considerably more money than you' creatures, or the psychologically challenged misfits who need to display their power like a frog puffing itself up to twice its size – I remember once watching Robert Maxwell preparing to be interviewed, and stretching out his hand, palm upward, in a rare moment of expectant and threatening silence. A grovelling flunkey carefully placed a cup of tea on it for the great man, but Maxwell barely glanced at it. 'Coffee!' he snapped, and the offending cup was silently spirited away and a fresh one substituted. It was barely sane. Maxwell had a passion for showing off, and we can all think of other people in public life, and probably at work, who suffer from a similar affliction – but for the rest of us, there are other ways of proving to ourselves and to other people that we are worth something.

Some people I have known who lost their jobs chose to demonstrate the skills of management and organisation that they had developed in their working lives in hardly noticeable ways, by running shops or small businesses for charities; others took entirely unsuitable jobs as assistant librarians or school crossing attendants just to show that they could maintain the discipline of going to work every day. Some took painting courses to develop hidden talents they had always believed they had. But the work doesn't have to be exciting or even useful: what we're considering here is rather the way it can be used to rebuild someone's self-esteem one brick at a time. For many of us, a sense of our own worth is inextricably tied up with what we can do – and, more importantly, with what other people *see* we can do. Losing your job can take away that reassurance, and winning it back is an important priority.

## ACCEPT IT?

Depression, the fourth neat category in the theorists' list, creeps up on all of us at some time or another – I certainly had my own down times, which I don't look back on with much pleasure – and we deal with it in our own ways. But there is still the fifth response to disaster, which is simply to accept it. That's a thought that occurs, however briefly, to the most determined salaryman as he faces the prospect of losing his job – that maybe, just maybe, he could sort out his affairs so that he doesn't have to go back to work at all.

It may start as just an idle fancy over a morning cup of coffee, but then it develops into hastily scribbled sums on the back of an envelope, then possibly into a spreadsheet on the computer, and maybe even to an appointment with a financial adviser. By the end of it, he has worked out that the pension contributions he's made already, together with a reduction in his lifestyle and a little bit of luck, should be enough to see him through; if it's an illness that's shattered his life into pieces, then he may well settle down to the calm, unhurried life of an invalid. And if it was the break-up of a relationship – well, he reckons he'll probably be better off on his own anyway. Reading a lot of books? Going to the movies? Maybe watching a lot of cricket matches, or just pottering around the garden – however he decides to spend his life, one answer to the challenge of freedom is to ditch a load of material ambitions and luxuriate in the quiet life that has, like all the best rewards he can remember, just fallen into his lap.

And if that sounds patronising and dismissive, then it's not supposed to. Mike, who was made redundant after a successful career as director of an international hotel company, started off with a determined effort to get back to the well-padded way of life he had known before the crash, sending off 70 job applications in a few months. He was desperate to get back onto his very comfortable treadmill, and his CV seemed to do the business: he got a dozen interviews, but no job offers. At the age of 47, he reckoned the reason was that he was too old for the young bucks who were interviewing him to see how useful he could be. Then he changed tack, setting up his own company – which he did very successfully. But something had changed: he was no longer prepared to put in the hours, the effort and the commitment that he had done before.

When he wrote to me, he was earning about half as much as he had done before, but revelling in the extra spare time and the ability to schedule his work to fit in with what he wants to do. 'I work the hours I choose, averaging about three days a week,' he said. 'This gives me time to stand at my bedroom window and watch birds – 34 species to date, including goldfinches, greenfinches, pheasants, and woodpeckers. Rare species I have seen include a brambling, a wryneck, a yellowhammer, and a goldcrest.'

He had practically forgotten life in the office, and he had long given up those old ambitions to tear up any more trees in the corporate jungle. On the downside, early retirement had become a pipedream, and he was no longer looking for a second home in France. 'But overall, I am less stressed, healthier and happier than I would be if I were doing the same job I had four years ago,' he said. Unlike him, I wouldn't know a wryneck from a brambling if they paraded in front of me with little labels round their necks. Birds don't excite me, which is probably my loss. But over the past few years, I have learned a little about how people respond to redundancy – and I have never heard a more upbeat, enthusiastic, enthralling description of the new life that is there to be grasped.

## THERE IS NO WAY BACK

Almost everyone plays each of these roles at different times. What is important, though, is to remember one of the two laws of the jungle: there is no way back. The struggle to find another job just like the one you left behind may be successful, but as you walk through the door of your new office, put your briefcase down on your new desk and turn with a sigh of satisfaction to your new PC, you will find that something has changed. Even if the job is more or less identical to the one you left behind, even though the new company may be just like the old one, *something* has changed. It's something you can't run away from – because what has changed is yourself.

Geoff had never thought of himself as particularly ruth-less as he climbed his company ladder from his early twen-ties. By the time he was in his mid-forties, he had a senior position, a great deal of respect, and the responsibility that goes with it. The salary, the car and the pension were all in place, and the regular holidays in North Africa, the USA, and the ski slopes of France all bore witness to a success-ful career. He had a fulfilling, exciting role in his company – and if the past few months had been stressful, as he called a succession of young executives into his office to tell them they were no longer needed, he told himself that was part of his job too. After all, he reasoned, the company had to do whatever was necessary to keep itself profitable, and they were well treated when they left.

And then, having handled all the redundancies, it was his turn. He hadn't seen it coming, though with hindsight he should have done: his department was being restructured, and there was no room for him in it.

He had a generous pay-off – but what he really wanted was the job and the recognition. The car and the holi-days would be nice too, of course, but the most important thing was to get back the sense of a role – the feeling that he was part of a wider organisation, with responsibil-ities and people relying on him. Within a few months, he was back at work, in a different company, with a slightly higher salary – the redundancy was behind him, like a bad dream, the only thing left of it the five-figure balance of his redundancy payment, which was still sitting in the bank. A good story, in fact, which leaves you thinking that things can work out pretty well. But it's even better than that.

'I'd changed,' he told me. 'The job was much the same, and all the conditions were as good as or better than I'd had before. But I'd lost the unquestioning loyalty to the company that I'd always had before. I go home a bit more, and work late a bit less now. So being pushed out had made me realise that I had to look after myself – but it also made me realise that I had to look after the people who worked for me as well as I could. I think I'm a better manager than I was as a result of the experience – and I know I'm a more relaxed person.'

Or another way to explain what I mean might be a story of my own, from when I was ill. I had bone marrow cancer, and the doctor explained to me that the one hope of getting rid of it was to have a transplant. My marrow would have to be killed with chemicals and radiation, and replaced with new marrow from a donor. The only catch was that once my own marrow was destroyed, if I didn't get the transplant, I would die. 'It's as if we were to throw you off a cliff, and then catch you before you fall,' he explained. I imagined, in my naïve way, that the best outcome I could hope for would be that I would walk away from this metaphorical cliff top cured – as good as new – but I was wrong. What happened was that the whole experience changed me: as I slowly got better, in the weeks that followed the transplant, I realised that I wasn't the person I had been before. I found different things funny, different things sad; food tasted different; my hair even grew back a different colour, for God's sake, and without the balding bits.

I'm not saying that redundancy is like cancer – in some ways, although the stakes aren't as high, it can be much more difficult, because all you have to do when you're lying flat-out in a hospital bed at the middle of a rat's nest of tubes is what you're told, whereas when you are dealing with redundancy, you have decisions to make, jobs to do and a life to get on with. But what is true is that both experiences change you. You won't necessarily find that redundancy is a cure for middle-aged baldness – it might be more popular if it were – but you may well find that it makes you a tougher, more self-reliant, less biddable employee.

That new toughness doesn't mean, incidentally, that your fangs will drip with blood as you savage the limp bodies of your erstwhile tormentors. I did say, a little while ago, that there were *two* immutable laws of the jungle: one, as I explained, was that there is no way back, but the other is that there is no room for revenge. There's no reason for it, come to that – after all, however cross you feel, no-one actually *owes* you a job.

That's not an argument for not having fun, and if letting down someone's tyres or arranging for large, exotic and embarrassing deliveries of intimate and anonymous gifts to their home address makes you feel that your sense of cosmic justice has been assuaged after you've been shown the door, then that might seem like a perfectly sensible investment of time and effort. Wronged wives, who may cut the arms off an erring husband's Savile Row suits, or distribute the cherished contents of his wine cellar around the doorsteps of the neighbourhood as if they were free gifts from the milkman, have more opportunity for vengeance than most newly redundant employees, but a little ingenuity works wonders. I heard one story, probably apocryphal, about a man who left his office computer with an instruction to send out hundreds of cards to the company's leading clients, wishing them the peace and love of Jesus at Christmas time, and inviting them to a roast turkey dinner. The cards went out in July, which would presumably have been rather puzzling to their recipients – even if the company hadn't been based in Jeddah, with most of its clients senior Saudi officials. They were even less impressed by the pictures of the baby Jesus on the front of the company card than they were by the invitation to roast turkey and plum pudding in the middle of a Saudi summer.

But however devious the scheme you think up may be, the catch is that it is only really rewarding if your one-time employers know that it was you who did it – and it is only really safe if they don't. Company legal departments are not known for their sense of humour, and so perhaps thoughts of complicated schemes of revenge are best confined to long, Byzantine fantasies as you lie awake at night, fuming. Few things sound less funny than a practical joke in court.

No, the best way to leave anything, whether it is a dinner party, a discussion or a well-paid job, is by closing the door quietly behind you, rather than slamming it so as to impress everyone with the force of your personality and the strength of your feelings. After all, you never know when you might want to open it again. If you've been thrown off your treadmill and out of your cage, then the soft click of that cage door closing gently behind you is the signal for the start of a new life. There may be no way back, but there are thousands of ways forward.

## NOTES

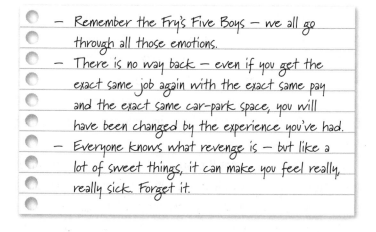

— Remember the Fry's Five Boys — we all go through all those emotions.

— There is no way back — even if you get the exact same job again with the exact same pay and the exact same car-park space, you will have been changed by the experience you've had.

— Everyone knows what revenge is — but like a lot of sweet things, it can make you feel really, really sick. Forget it.

# Chapter Three

## Always Look on the . . .

**B**right side of life. That was the advice in Monty Python's *Life of Brian* – although if you really do ... start to whistle as you cast an eye over your P45 and take a large mouthful of life's gristle, you are likely to be hauled off by the men in white coats before you've reached the end of the first bar. But don't panic – although it's also a pretty fair rule of thumb that when anyone in authority says that to you, whether it's a policeman, the Prime Minister or just the guy who looks after the car-park, you should start running and not stop until you've reached a high enough hill to look down from in safety on whatever is about to go wrong.

In short, there is often something suspect about people who point out that there is a silver lining to every cloud. It's usually the last desperate cry before they give up – and in any case, those of us who are either more neurotic or more realistic know that the reverse is also true: every silver lining has a cloud hiding away somewhere behind it. But even so . . .

## THE ADVANTAGES OF BEING IN MY FIFTIES (THIS IS A VERY SHORT SECTION)

We're all supposed to envy young people – but if you have to be made redundant at some time in your life (and in-creasing numbers of people are likely to be over the next few decades) then there are advantages to having it hap-pen in your fifties rather than your twenties or thirties. 'The first time I was out of work, I was in my thirties, and I didn't know what had hit me,' said one friend, in those shell-shocked days after I'd started to look around at how the world had changed now that I didn't have a job. 'For ten years, I had been moving easily from job to job in the engineering industry because the economy was expanding, and there were any number of opportunities for people with my qualifications. So it was a shock when I left one job and found myself still out of work six months later. It was a difficult time for me, because I simply hadn't expected it.'

But when the same thing happened 20 years later – with the important difference that this time he was pushed rather than stepping calmly overboard – he found it much easier to handle. 'I had much better tools to deal with it this time around. My expectations were more realistic, and I knew what it was going to be like. I could anticipate the times when I would be feeling down, which made it much easier to cope with them,' he said. 'I was in a situation that I knew and understood, not trying to fight my way through in the dark.'

And anyway, there are a lot of things to enjoy about not having a regular job.

## PUTTING MY FEET UP (IN MORE WAYS THAN ONE)

There's the duck pond, for a start. Half a mile or so from where I live, there is a pond, with a tree next to it and a small island in the middle where a couple of ducks have their slightly Beatrix Potterish home in a little wooden shed. I had always been too busy to notice it before, although I knew it was there – but one day about a week into my new life, as I was composing yet more letters asking for work, I paused in my manic hammering of the keyboard and suddenly thought I would go for a walk for half an hour. There was a very enjoyable frisson of guilty pleasure as I closed the front door behind me – something I hadn't felt since bunking off school occasionally 40 years ago – and I strolled up the main road to turn into the field. And there, sitting on their island like the king and queen, were the ducks.

But there were not just two: this time, there was a large bundle of fluffy brown feathers snuggled up together on the bank just next to them, looking as if someone had emptied the contents of a duvet onto the grass. As I stood there, one of the ducks flopped heavily into the water, and the large fluffy bundle gradually broke up into thirteen smaller shapeless feathery blobs. I mentioned before that birds don't excite me – but this was something different. I sat down and leant against the tree in the sunshine to watch as the thirteen, one by one, joined their parent – I don't know enough about ducks to know if it was their mother or their father – in the water. My snatched half an hour turned into an hour. And then an hour and a half. It was two full hours before I was back at my desk – and do you know what? I didn't feel the least bit guilty. How many jobs can you think of where you can take a couple of hours off in the middle of the day to go and watch the ducks? That afternoon is one I shall remember for the rest of my life – and I've already forgotten what letters they were I was supposed to be writing.

Or instead of putting your feet up as you watch the world go by, you can always put them up on one of the exercise machines at the gym. Within a few months of losing my job, I realised that since I hadn't had to struggle in to the office, I had been going to the gym more often than I could remember for years. It was a revelation. In the middle of the day, there were none of the fit young twenty-somethings about to make me feel inferior with their pounding of the treadmills for six hours at a time and lifting weights like two-ton trucks above their heads – they were away terrorising their innocent office staff with their snarling cartoon impersonations of alpha-males. Back in the gym, I could potter about at my own easygoing pace with the other unemployed blokes and the housewives. How effective it was, I'm not sure – when I did go in during the evening, my son would occasionally stroll past with the supercilious smile of a man of 24, and observe that the last person to pick up the weights I was sweating blood over wore plaits and a gymslip. But it felt good, even if you have to take my claims of being super-fit at 50-plus with a large pinch of low-sodium flavouring agent.

If my sweaty mornings on the treadmill and struggling with weights like millstones had been aimed at sculpting a torso like Brad Pitt's out of my saggy 50-odd-year-old body, then they would have been a failure. In fact, someone told me so one morning, as I paused between sessions. It may have been God, or it may have been my imagination, or it may even conceivably have been the gym manager, but I heard a deep, resonant voice speaking in my head, in much the same way as the Old Testament prophets must have done. 'Don't be such a jerk,' it said – if it was God, then he had clearly decided to adopt a 21st-century teenage vernacular, instead of the thee's and thou's more commonly associated with him.

'Don't be such a jerk. You are not Sir Steve Redgrave. There are different rules for him, but you are 52, and however many times you push that lump of metal up into the air, you will never be 51 again.' And he paused. Then, almost as an afterthought, he added: 'In fact, if you try to push it into the air much more, you will probably never be 53 either.' So, carefully avoiding the mirror in the changing room as I dressed, I settled for a shower (a warm one – I may not be very bright, but I'm not that stupid) and a rub down, and went for a toasted bacon and tomato sandwich.

The days when I fantasised about looking like Michelangelo's David are long gone. If I wanted to stand stark naked on a block of marble in a Florentine gallery to be stared at by the tourists, there might be some point in it, but for my ordinary day-to-day slobbing about in jeans and a tee-shirt (but no suit!), walking to the shops or having a pint in the pub, it would probably be a bit of a waste of time and effort. I realised a long time ago that the only six-pack I would ever possess now was the sort I can pick up from the off-licence. And anyway, that wasn't why I was at the gym.

Going there was about reasserting control over one small aspect of my life. I might have gone to yoga classes instead, or learned a language, or started growing chrysanthemums; all that mattered was that it was something that I wanted to do, and I was in charge of it. My former bosses might have made me redundant, but the upside of that was that they couldn't stop me now from doing what I wanted. There are all sorts of ways you can take control, in all sorts of situations: going into hospital for chemotherapy, you shave your hair off, because if it's coming off, then *I'm* going to take it off; come out of a divorce settlement with a lot less money than you expected, and you book yourself a holiday, because however much there may or may not be, what there is left is *yours*. In just the same way, when you're suddenly given a lot more time off than you want or than you know what to do with, you fill it with stuff that *you* want to do – just because you can. Going to the gym more often may seem to be a trivial example of taking charge of your life, but it's one that a lot of people choose. You weren't in control when they took your job away, and it's important to be back in control now.

## WHAT AM I WORTH?

The gym is also a way of answering one of the questions that crop up after you get that fax, letter, text message or whatever else those fearless executives use when they want to tell you that it's time to go, but don't have the guts to do it to your face. If 'What am I going to do?' is the first, then 'What am I worth?' comes pretty soon after it.

'What am I worth?' you ask yourself, very quietly and privately. Not necessarily in terms of what you have in the bank, although that may well be the first thing that occurs to most people – for the lucky ones, the employment laws might mean that they may have more spare cash piled up there after they are made redundant than they have ever had before or will have again. I have one friend, a talented and amusing accountant (and those aren't words that often go together) who tells me that he has made more money out of his house and his redundancy cheques than he has earned in the last ten years. He is a happy and relaxed man.

But for most of us, redundancy is a terrifying financial prospect. That's a topic that we'll come to later, but for now, the 'What am I worth?' question deals rather with how you value yourself. One of the hardest readjustments that you have to make is to change the feeling that the value other people put on you is the most important part of your life.

And it's not just other people: it's very easy, as you stare at the words on the page or listen to the silky platitudes that tell you your job has just gone up the spout, to start to doubt your own worth, and it's important to do whatever you can to avoid falling into that trap. Another friend called Chris – not my former colleague from the office; he wouldn't mind my saying that he is much older and less good-looking than she is – told me that he had completed a series of psychometric tests when he was looking for a job ten years ago. 'They told me I would be fitted for work in civil engineering, computing or project management, which was quite impressive, as those were the areas I had spent my career in – but it was hardly a lot of help,' he said.

'But they also gave me a series of IQ tests, in which I came in the top 1% of their clients. That made me feel a bit better, and I applied to join Mensa as a result. To be honest,

I found Mensa a complete waste of time – but the buzz of being accepted for a society which describes its members having IQs in the top 2% of the population certainly gave my self-esteem a boost at a time when it needed it.'

## HITTING THE PHONES

I had a different technique to assuage my battered ego. I used the phone and, incidentally, got a disproportionate amount of childish pleasure from the fact that my soon-to-be-ex employers were paying the bill. The fax I'd got had given me about three weeks' notice – probably less than I was entitled to under law, but hey, who was counting now? After all, my lawyer had told me that going to court would probably cost me more than I would be likely to get out of any court case. I worked the three weeks – pre-dictably without any great enthusiasm, but out of a sense of pride and because I wanted to shut that door behind me gently – and I did take the opportunity to bash their phones. The office phone bill probably showed a significant spike during that month as I rang everyone I could think of.

These calls weren't the same as the ones I'd made in the days immediately after my redundancy: then, I had been calling the people I know best, because they are the best ones to turn to in a crisis. Your mates make you feel better – even those like the one who said I'd always been redundant anyway. Then, I'd been looking for a bit of friendship and reassurance – but now, I was calling people who I thought might be able to help me find a new job. Or rather, since

I was already beginning to realise that I didn't just want more of what I'd been having for the last 30 years, people who I thought might be able to help me find a new life.

There were some people on my list that I'd known for years, but there were also acquaintances, contacts, and even one or two people I thought I could pretend I'd met, though I never had. I wrote lists of friends, lists of people I'd met through work, lists of people I'd been recommended to call, and lists of the lists I'd made and gradually, over that three-week period, I ticked off the names one by one.

I wasn't asking for another job – I didn't know yet if I wanted to take another full-time post anywhere, and anyway, that's the sort of question that outfaces the best of friends. Unless you happen to have Roman Abramovich or Bill Gates in your address book, there aren't many people in the world who can fit you into their employment plans just because you're a nice guy. Or at least, if there are, then either the jobs they are offering aren't worth taking, or you shouldn't be reading this book. Put it down at once and go check your share options, buy another Aston Martin, or just count your money and thank your lucky stars.

In fact, I did ring one old friend to ask for a job. He was the boss of a big company, and I thought I'd pitch an idea to him about how I could do some PR work for him. Ringing him was hell, simply because although I'd always liked him a lot, and we'd known each other for a long time, we weren't often in touch, so it was pretty obvious that I was phoning to ask him for a favour, which wasn't a particularly comfortable feeling. But he was great – took me out to lunch, said all the right sympathetic things, and even suggested a couple of people in his organisation I could talk to about my idea – and I never phoned them. He must have thought I was either ungrateful or stupid – but it was slightly more complicated than that. I know now, and I think, deep down, I knew then, that I am no more a PR man than I am a professional figure-skater. My idea was madness – it would have ended in tears.

But I shall never forget what he did for me over lunch. Never mind finding me a possible job – he gave me a good shot of confidence. He treated me like a grown-up, like someone who had some ideas and had something to contribute, rather than the washed-up and incompetent old hack I was starting to feel like. It was the best thing he could have done, and one day, given the chance, I shall do the same sort of thing for someone else.

On a more severely practical level, what I wanted from the people I knew with connections in the media was ideas of people I could call to find a few sticking-plaster jobs that might tide me over financially, until I'd worked out what I wanted to do with the rest of my life. The old friend who had been so cross when he found that I wasn't dying of cancer came up trumps, for instance, and suggested a couple of other places I might call. That's not something to sniff at, incidentally – apart from the money that you need, finding someone who is willing to pay you is a great boost for the battered ego.

Those tips were certainly useful as far as they went – but the real point of all the phone calls was to talk to people who knew me about what they thought I might be best suited for. I wasn't just looking for a new job, I was looking for a new future, so it made sense to talk to the people who knew me best. In doing so, I found out something else in passing that gave me a lot of encouragement: by and large, they weren't that sympathetic about what I thought was my plight. They didn't think I was so unlucky.

## A CHANCE FOR SOMETHING NEW?

I knew already that there were a lot of people who were made redundant, one way or another, in their late forties or early fifties, either through early retirement or, rather more brutally, in the way that I had been – but what I hadn't realised was just how many there are who are still in work, but dream wistfully about what might be. That silent army of the discontented was even bigger than I had realised. Maybe they had reached as far as they were going to go, and were just marking time until they could retire; maybe the enthusiasm, the drive, the adventure that had powered them through their twenties and thirties had simply ebbed away; maybe, whatever the law said about ageism, their employers just didn't believe that people who could remember when the Beatles were lovable mop-tops could still hack it in the age of the internet and the iPod. Everyone enjoys security – but there were a lot of people out there who saw my redundancy as a chance to do something new that I ought to grab as hard as I could. Something, in fact, to envy.

That was easy enough for them, of course; they weren't the ones with the mortgage to pay and the children to see through university. But it was a reassuring start: there was a positive view to be taken. For many of us, from our very first day at work, the job begins to take over our soul. It is at the centre of our lives, the measure of our achievements, and the top priority when it comes to sorting out what we do, where we go and whom we meet. That may change imperceptibly slowly, like the sun setting, but – unless you are unbelievably unlucky – it does change. You often don't even see it start to happen: one very good friend, made redundant after 30 years spent climbing various ladders, was very touched when his children bought him and his wife a picnic hamper to celebrate their wedding anniversary, along with a couple of tickets for an outdoor theatre production. As the two of them sat in the park on a summer evening, sipping white wine and tucking into the food their children had put in the hamper, he was talking enthusiastically about his plans to get back into corporate life again. Was that simple professional ambition, or was there mixed up in it a desire to get his revenge – a sense that he'd show them what a good man they had lost? Probably a bit of both – but he was certainly anxious to get back into the cage and onto the treadmill again as fast as he could.

His wife, though – who had a successful career of her own – was a bit more quiet and thoughtful. Then, in one of the short pauses in his almost manic professional enthusiasm, she spoke. 'Do you realise, this is the first time we've had a picnic like this for more than 20 years?' she said – and his brief pause stretched out into a long silence. 'It's worth thinking about,' she went on, as she took his hand. 'You can only drive one car; you can only go on so many holidays; you can only wear one suit. What are we doing all this for?' She was wrong about the suit, of course – once you've jumped off the treadmill, you don't even need one – but she was right about everything else. She changed her job too, shortly afterwards, and they moved to a smaller house in a cheaper area. Now he works from home, earning a lot less and living a lot more.

Someone else I knew was made redundant from a teaching job when his college was reorganised and his job vanished. He was in his early forties, and his career and his prospects seemed to have vanished. For a couple of months he was plunged in despair – and then he started looking around for supply teaching contracts, and then for work as an examiner. Now, a few years on, he oversees examiners all over the country, earns at least as much as he did before, and works more or less as he likes. He'll retire gradually, just taking jobs when it suits him: the man who pushed him out – whom he would cheerfully have strangled just a few years ago – did him a big favour.

I may not be that bright, but even I can't write these stories without remembering what I said earlier – that cheery remarks about clouds and silver linings are often just whistling in the dark, the prelude to crushing despair. The ship often gives a few cheery blasts on its horn just before it ploughs into the iceberg. But the point about the people I spoke to, and the readers who wrote to the *Aftershock* column, was that they weren't claiming to have found something to make up for what they had lost – in many cases, they were saying they had found something better than they had before. It wasn't just a silver lining they were claiming to have found, but silver all the way through.

## JUMPING SHIP

In any case, not everyone needs that brutal push to realise that they aren't happy at work – and they don't necessarily need to jump ship to start to put things right. By the time we get to our late forties, many of us are simply turning over in neutral – doing what we're doing, just because that's what we do. We work competently, reliably and without the slightest spark of enthusiasm. But, we keep telling ourselves, it pays the mortgage. We can't afford to give it up. It might get better; and anyway, nobody else could do it quite like we do. It's not necessarily about pay, or about working conditions, or pension, or any of the objective aspects of the job we have. Sometimes, we just *feel* that it's wrong.

I spoke, for instance, to a man called Tom, who worked in the City. He had a six-figure salary, he made his own management decisions, and he had lots of esteem and respect from his colleagues – but, like most things that sound too good to be true, it was, at least if you asked him. He worked on the trading floor at an international bank, selling derivatives and other pieces of paper that make some people very rich without anyone quite understanding how. Tom, of course, wasn't his real name, since not liking your job is not at all the same thing as wanting to be sacked.

'I feel increasingly dissatisfied with my role,' he said. 'I'm constantly under pressure, and I see no way out. It's becoming more and more cut-throat. What used to be a fun job with some very like-minded colleagues is becoming a drain, and I am starting to fear Monday mornings – something I have never done.' He wondered about teaching, or maybe taking a job in a small company where he might get less money, but where his experience would be valued. Well, it's hard to dredge up much sympathy for a man with a job description like his, and my first thought was that I should be so lucky as to be dissatisfied with £100,000 or more. But then I thought of the job I'd left behind, and the regular trudge into an office I didn't want to go to, and realised how similar Tom's position was to the one I'd been in – leaving aside the £100,000, of course – and I thought how much I'd regretted not getting out of an unrewarding job much sooner than I had. I didn't say this, because despite appearances, I'm not that stupid, but my immediate, private thought was, 'Jump, mate, before you're pushed! Find yourself something you enjoy, and do that instead.'

Not for the first time in my life, though, I found myself in a minority of one. Everyone else he spoke to was suggesting that he should look for ways to change the way his present job worked, rather than chuck it in the bin. If he went to his employers and said how unfulfilling he was finding the work, one employment consultant said, they might simply tell him to go – but on the other hand, they might just take steps to help him put it right. That, of course, was advice that was particularly worth listening to because of where it came from. If he'd jacked his job in on the spot, he would have been another potential client for the consultant – advice is always more convincing when it's against the interests of the person giving it.

And I guess the cautious warning to think again was right. I'm all in favour of burning the suit, but it can be chilly until the fire gets going. It's foolish to stay in a job that you don't find rewarding and fulfilling any more, but it's even more foolish to throw everything away without looking carefully at possible ways of making it better. The very act of considering a move and looking at the different options you have is important. You may decide to stay in the job that you're in, but you will be staying there because you've made a positive decision, rather than because you're just trundling around in the treadmill. You've taken control.

Perhaps you sometimes need a second pair of eyes to look at the pros and cons of changing your job. Chewing things over with your partner, your friends or your family is usually a good move: after all, if you decide to jump ship, you're going to want them in the life raft with you. Certainly, like everything else, coping with redundancy is easier if there is more than one of you to do it. In a way, starting a new life is less frightening when you have no-one but yourself to think about – but when you have a partner or a family, it's a team challenge. Often, partners may be more worried than the person whose job has gone. They have a straightforward practical role, of course – it's much easier to make choices if you have a wife or husband bringing in a salary all the time – but it's also important to reach joint decisions about the future. The new life you are trying to find, after all, whether it's in your old job, in a new one, or in no job at all, is one that you will be sharing.

## NOTES

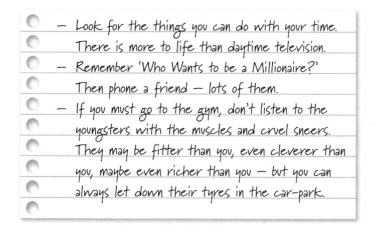

— Look for the things you can do with your time.
There is more to life than daytime television.
— Remember 'Who Wants to be a Millionaire?'
Then phone a friend — lots of them.
— If you must go to the gym, don't listen to the
youngsters with the muscles and cruel sneers.
They may be fitter than you, even cleverer than
you, maybe even richer than you — but you can
always let down their tyres in the car-park.

# Chapter Four

## Looking for Help

I t was time to find some help.

Back there in the treetops of the jungle that was work, I dimly remembered, where alpha-plus males swing from the trees beating their chests, baring their teeth, and giving challenging mating calls, help was something you occasionally offered other people when you were feeling particularly kindly disposed. It gave you a nice warm glow when you stood up for an old lady on the tube, or suggested kindly to a young colleague in the newsroom that the caption 'Foreign general standing as if he had a brush stuffed up his backside' might raise a few eyebrows when placed underneath a photograph of the Japanese ambassador. (That example is true, I promise you: there can be a dangerous sense-of-humour gap between work-experience youngsters and the companies they serve.)

But help certainly wasn't something you ever wanted anyone to suspect you might need yourself. Asking for it was tantamount to admitting that you weren't really up to the job – volunteering for last place in the sack-race. Being a good loser is all very well in theory, but how many of us actually want to claim that role? Who wants to be thought of as a self-confessed failure? And I don't think for a moment that these worries apply only to men: in my experience, the female sex sorts these things out at a slightly younger age – say about 12 – but those armour-plated young women with hard smiles that you occasionally bump into in bars that are much too expensive for you – what you might term the female alpha-males – clearly suffer from the same testosterone fixation as their male colleagues. Open a door for them and you risk a sharp jab of beautifully manicured fingers in your eyes and a hack on the shins as they defend their reputations as snarling big beasts of the jungle. Far better to avoid them and admit that, for those of us down here on the forest floor, things are different.

## THE BIGGEST, SIMPLEST, HARDEST QUESTION

I think it's something you grow into – the acceptance that looking after yourself might involve recognising that you sometimes need help, and not being too proud to go and ask for it. Taking the first step is important, whether it is going to the employment service, or simply buying yourself a book about the problem that you're facing. What you're doing is admitting that you have a problem that you can't handle alone.

At an earlier difficult time in my life, an old, wise friend once asked me two questions. 'Who do you think you are – Superman?' was the first, by which he meant that I should stop being so pig-headed and admit that I could do with a helping hand. But the second was even simpler and even harder: 'What do you want?' It's a simple question, and one of the commonest you'll ever be asked, but it's also one of the hardest to answer. It's one that faces us constantly as children, and one that we're never supposed to ask ourselves. If you answer it honestly, you are often called selfish, and as a result, many of the pleasantest people you'll meet never sit down and think about it.

What do *you* want?
What do you *want*?

It's the biggest question of all. Not 'What do you need?' Not 'What do you think you ought to want?' Not 'What would you like to want?' Not 'What do other people think you want?' Not even 'What can you get?' and certainly not 'What is it easiest to settle for?' but simply 'What do *you* want?' 'What do you *want*?' There had been no shortage of advice from the first few days after I'd got my marching orders – and one thing everyone seemed to agree on was that before I could set out on the search for a new job, let alone a new life, I had to sit down and work out a coherent game plan. But to have a game plan, I had to have an objective. And to have an objective, I had to answer that question.

What did I want?

## THE PROFESSIONALS – A SCEPTIC'S GUIDE

I had turned to my friends earlier not just for support in the pub of the 'Isn't it awful?' kind, but also for contacts, suggestions, and job ideas. They could help with that question too – but their help was limited by the fact that they *were* friends. You're not always the best person to answer that important question all on your own: you may need some help in seeing past the trees to get a good view of the wood. On your own, it's all too tempting to go for the easy option, to settle for the choice that is going to be less trouble to take. But though you know that, by and large, your mates are on your side – and when you're reeling from the first big hit, that's not something to undervalue – they're not going to push you or challenge you. And pushing and challenging is what you need now.

So what about the professionals? A glance around the internet shows that there is no shortage of companies wanting to put your life in order, and there were plenty of volunteers out there all too eager to make my mind up for me for a fee – counsellors, outplacement agencies, and career coaches; sorting people out is a growth industry. Over a period, I think I tasted most of the bottles of snake oil they had for sale. Trouble is, like the shysters peddling oddball cures for cancer, they seem to range from the simply avaricious ones who just want to get their hands on your money to the amiably nutty, who would have you sitting under a crystal pyramid and humming with your eyes shut and your head in a damp towel. They all have their uses, no doubt – but my problem was that I had always been instinctively suspicious of professional tree-hugging and do-goodery. The ones who wanted to charge me money seemed to be circling like sharks, while the ones who didn't – well, my old Yorkshire grandfather would have written them off with a shrug as 'nutty as squirrel muck in a walnut farm'. Any alpha-male back there in the jungle of work would tell you that trees are for swinging from, not hugging.

But then, I suspect, my grandfather and I were both a bit out-of-date, as grandfathers and men in their fifties tend to be: like everything else, you get out of companies like that what you put in. Counsellors, for instance, will suggest ways to get you back on track after an emotional upheaval, but I heard a bizarre story from one friend who went to see one as his marriage fell apart around him. The two of them would sit in silence across the fireplace from each other, looking at each other thoughtfully for precisely an hour, before my friend wrote the charming old gent a cheque for £50 for the privilege. The counsellor told him after one of these buttock-clenchingly embarrassing sessions that his silence was not simply silence. My friend's refusal to speak apparently spoke volumes about his inner turmoil, he said – but my friend thought to himself as he wrote out the weekly cheque that what it was really saying was that he must be crackers enough to eat cheese off to hand over his money like this. Not a good experience.

## A KNIGHT IN SHINING ARMOUR

Fifty pounds – and not tax-deductible either, I might add – seemed like a high price for my friend to pay for an hour spent staring at his feet and wondering whether he ought to tell a joke – but it was a bargain offer compared with the first professional I visited myself. In fact, it all started about as well as it possibly could have done. He must have been one of the nicest men I'd ever met, a true knight in shining armour, it seemed – and it was the purest chance that he had ridden into my life just when I needed him most. I'd been sitting at my computer writing one of my scores of letters, when a pop-up message appeared in front of me as if by magic. In the olden days, God might have sent an archangel or a fiery pillar, but in the 21st century, when he wasn't passing on messages in the gym, he was clearly internet-savvy and abreast of the latest tools of mass communication. Sweetly, it honestly never occurred to me that accessing some internet-site or other might have sent my details winging silently to some company that would follow up this valuable tip-off to find a new potential customer. Even less did I imagine that one of the companies I had incautiously given my email address to might have sold it on to make a few quid on the side. Naïve, me? I reckoned I was simply the lucky recipient of a coincidental twist of fate. Contact this website, said my divinely inspired pop-up – so I did. After that, it took me just a couple of phone calls, and there I was, sitting in his office, like a fly smiling at the spider . . . who lounges back comfortably in his web, without a care in the world.

We all like being told that we're exceptional, and I suppose I'm no exception. And when the person who is praising you to the skies goes on to suggest that nobody else really understands or appreciates you – that, if you'll beg my pardon, people have been taking advantage of your talents and your good nature for years – then you realise that you are in the presence of quite remarkable perception. My new friend even gave me a set of puzzles to do to prove how bright and alert and intelligent I was, and then sat back and listened appreciatively while I told him about myself. Is there a person on the planet who can resist talking about themselves to someone who clearly wants to listen? If there is, it's not me.

And then, after sitting back and nodding sagely as I listed my accomplishments in case he had missed anything, he started. It was like the old joke, 'Well, that's enough about me, let's talk about you. What do you think about me?' – but in reverse. All he seemed to do was to talk about me and how clever and talented I was. If I hadn't been such a trusting person, I might almost have thought that I was being flattered. He was, to be fair, quite astonishingly perceptive. It was, he said, amazing that I did not have a job – scandalous that some big company had not snapped me up before I had finished reading my old employer's fax message, and recruited me for some undefined but extremely senior post on the spot, commensurate with my talents. And, he added, they would have offered me a rate of pay vastly superior to that I had been limping along with in my old job. 'Because,' he confided, leaning towards me across his desk, 'you do realise you are slightly off the pace when it comes to pay, don't you?'

Well, that attracted my attention again, although I must admit that it was starting to wander at this point – even I can only take so much praise at any one time. I glanced around his office. Oddly, there didn't seem to be any photographs, or books, or files anywhere. Not even a pen – just a telephone which never rang, and the paper cups of rapidly cooling coffee which he had fetched for us from the little kitchen just down the corridor. It might almost have been an office which he'd hired for the day – and now I came to think about it, there had been no company name-plate in the foyer downstairs. And the receptionist hadn't seemed to recognise his name when I had asked for him.

But who was I to be sceptical? Put simply, this nice, friendly man was offering me a job. Or at least, he was offering to find me one – and by God, I needed his help, as he was just explaining to me, with statistics carefully chosen to make my blood turn to ice. If I had been swimming in the sea, he would have been sitting in a boat smiling at me, and reminding me that I was in danger of drowning. 'One in three people over 50 are out of work – and by the time you get to 55, that figure has gone up to 50 per cent,' he told me. But luckily, he beamed like Mr Pickwick, I had a new friend. He was going to tell me where I could find a new job, and probably help me choose from the sheaves of offers that would drop through my letter-box. All I had to do – he smiled with his mouth slightly open, looking slightly less Pickwickian and flexing his fingers slightly, a little like a spider might flex its legs before pouncing on its prey – all I had to do was to sign just *here* – he pushed a sheet of paper towards me – and agree to pay just £4,000 for his services . . .

The mention of £4,000 woke me like a bucket of cold water from the daydream into which his friendly voice and the warmth of the office had lulled me. From the tone of his voice, £4,000 didn't sound like a lot of money to him, but to me, it sounded like quite a large slice of my not-particularly-big final cheque. And I wasn't quite clear what he was going to do for it. When I pointed this out to him, he looked hurt and rather surprised, as if I had slapped him. This, clearly, was not the way one friend should speak to another.

Most important of all, he said, he would give me access to the hundreds of jobs – 'senior positions', he called them, in the same way that estate agents never say 'house' when 'desirable property' will do. These positions, he said, never make it to the appointments pages of the newspapers.

It still wasn't clear to me why companies who wanted to hire staff would do it in secret, and even less clear why they should choose to involve my friend Spiderman in their search – but there was more to come. The only guarantee, as far as I could see, was that he would give me some advice about writing a CV, coach me for interviews like my mum used to do when I was at school, and make a few phone calls on my behalf. He would organise a strategy for me. He would give me more personality tests to help me decide what I really wanted to do. He would, it was clear, promise to do practically anything if only I would hand over that cheque. All that support may be an attractive option when it's offered to you for nothing as part of your redundancy package – and if nothing else, it probably makes the bloated plutocrat who fired you feel a bit better about himself – but it's another matter when the money has to come out of your own shrinking bank account.

But he was ready for that one. After all, he smiled, leaning back in his chair as he added the clinching line, £4,000 was as nothing compared to the regular monthly income he was promising to find for me. A couple of weeks' pay – maybe a month's. That was all he was asking. If I was serious about wanting a job, it was a no-brainer – and if I wasn't, well, his shrug said it all. It was a choice between being a thrusting, determined professional and a sad, penny-pinching loser.

I've already confessed to being naïve. Long ago, when I was born, I'm told, the midwife noticed a small mark in the middle of my forehead. Over the next few months, it gradually developed into a large sign which said 'SUCKER', and ever since, I have been fair game for every passing con-man, card-sharp, and chiseller. If there is a car so old, broken-down and rusty that nobody is interested in it, the salesman simply has to send for me and he has done a deal. I am so gullible that I am convinced by party political broadcasts; I buy bottles of expensive designer scent from men with suitcases in the street who are offering it at knock-down bargain prices, and then I am regularly surprised when they smell like paint thinners. I am the man that advertising executives dream of. Why, I even believed the Labour party manifesto of 1997 – but even for me, this was, as my new friend had said, a no-brainer. Thanks, but no thanks.

I'm probably being unfair on him: to be fair, he gave me a couple of phone numbers of satisfied clients to ring, and they did indeed have nothing but good to say about his abilities and the service he offered. He would hardly be likely to have given me numbers for people who thought they'd wasted their money, of course, but he had clearly helped someone. But the deal with most recruitment consultants is that the company which is doing the hiring also does the paying. If he really had a bulging file of jobs that were suitable for me, and if I really couldn't find them by scouring the papers, then I probably missed a golden opportunity, but I didn't think so then, and I don't think so now. What I suspect I would actually have been paying for was someone to hold my hand, and give me the reassurance I wanted that I really was trying to do all I could to find a new job. It struck me as I walked away that you can buy an awful lot of hand-holding and sympathy for £4,000, and from even more attractive people than my friend with the glittering eyes and spider's web.

## THE COACH'S TALE

The next person who offered to help me was more believable, not least because she wasn't promising to find me a job, or even introduce me to lists of probably mythical potential employers. All she would do, she said, was help me find the answer to that crucial question. What did I want? I must admit that it was a recommendation as far as I was concerned that she had been through some of the same hoops that I had – and not only that, but had had much the same reaction to them. She had been made redundant a few years earlier by a caring, sharing employer right in the middle of a series of family crises. 'Every day for a year I walked past his car, and every day I wanted to let down his tyres,' she said, and I knew then that we might be talking the same language. Part of me wanted to ask his address and go round to do the job that she'd shied away from, but I just nodded and listened.

She had her own coaching business, and was, not surprisingly, more sanguine than I was about the whole get-you-back-on-your-feet industry. I must admit that I wasn't quite sure what the difference was between a coach and a counsellor – just a different plate on the door, it seemed to me. Well, I was wrong – and I found out in passing that the two don't like being confused. It's as bad as thinking that a New Zealander is an Australian, or a Canadian comes from the USA. Put simply, if counsellors look at the past and try to help you sort out the reasons why something has happened, coaches will claim to concentrate on the future and what you can do about it.

Ideally, my new friend said, most people would benefit from bits of each sort of advice at different times – from visits to counsellors, placement agencies, and career coaches. (I swallowed the temptation to suggest that they would have to be so wealthy to manage that sort of support network that they wouldn't need to work anyway.) 'But the crucial thing about coaching is that it digs the answers out from inside you – the coach doesn't tell you anything, but helps you to work out your own ideas,' she said.

So we had a go, sitting in a coffee bar in London – not the most conventional place for a professional consultation, but I had rather been put off office meetings by my brush with the spider's web. She pushed and probed, and wouldn't take 'I don't know' for an answer, and I tried to sketch out on a piece of paper how I thought I would like my life to pan out. I dredged my mind to try and think of times I could tell her about when I had felt really fulfilled and really successful, and I struggled to describe how I would like my life to look in five and ten years' time – and after 90 minutes or so, I did have some clearer ideas of what steps I wanted to take. How practical they were, I'm not sure – and as she said, it would take me a few more sessions to sort that out. She wouldn't be specific about how much I would have to pay in the long run – her clients tended to be companies, she said, and the money they pay has no relation to the amount a private client like me would have to find. A little bit of digging around suggested that other coaches were charging around £750 for a series of a dozen 45-minute telephone conversations, which seemed to me to be going it a bit for a chat on the phone, even by the standards of my teenage daughters.

But the fact that I didn't go back for more certainly doesn't mean that I wasn't impressed by what we achieved, because I was. I think an initial healthy scepticism is a good place to start from, but I'd have no hesitation about suggesting that other people should find themselves a career coach they can get on with, either off the internet, through personal recommendation, or by going to one of the coaching associations. After all, if they work, any of the professional deals on offer would seem worthwhile, and coaching seemed to me to be by far the most productive. My feeling is that getting the right coach – someone you can respond to on a personal level – is crucial. And I'm absolutely certain that you have to sort out very clearly in advance what you pay and exactly what you get. But I walked away because it wasn't for me – I guess when it comes to asking strangers for help, I'm my grandfather's grandson, and a bit of a grumpy old man. If you don't buy into it all with enthusiasm, you don't get the big rewards.

The way I assess the help that's on offer from people who want money from me is this – the more they offer, the less I believe. What impressed me about the conversation with a career coach was how *little* she said she could achieve. She didn't claim to be able to find me a job, she couldn't tell me what job to look for, and she wasn't about to draw up a detailed job-seeking strategy for me to follow. But what she could – and did – do was listen as I tried to stumble through my own half-thought-out ideas about what I wanted from my life, and ask me occasional questions to help me bring my ideas into focus. What she'd taught me, like all the best teachers, was something which I think I'd known all along without realising it.

But the most productive piece of advice I heard came, like most of the best things in life, from an old mate, over a drink. 'Happiness isn't rocket science,' he said. 'Find out what you enjoy doing most, and do more of it. And then work out what makes you unhappy, and stop doing it.' Well, maybe it's not quite that simple – after all, you can't spend all your time eating cream buns and watching 24 on the telly, and you can't just stop washing your car. But it was a good thought, which cost me only the price of a pint and a packet of crisps. I carefully stored it away for the future.

You can't escape this one. If being made redundant is a second chance, then to take it, you have to think through the answer to that single, over-riding question that I mentioned before. What do you want? If, like most people, you've never thought of thinking as work, then you'll get a shock with this one, because turning that question over and over in your mind will wear you out. But there is no short-cut. What do you want? Some of the answers may be surprising, even frightening, but you have to work your way through to them – and in the end, you have to do it yourself. The placement agencies may be able to help you find new jobs, although I don't believe they are as good at it as they claim, and the coaches and counsellors may put the question in different ways, and offer strategies for reaching a conclusion. Even wise old men like my mate in the pub can help – but only one person can find the answer.

## NOTES

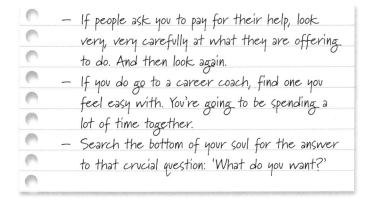

— If people ask you to pay for their help, look very, very carefully at what they are offering to do. And then look again.

— If you do go to a career coach, find one you feel easy with. You're going to be spending a lot of time together.

— Search the bottom of your soul for the answer to that crucial question: 'What do you want?'

# Chapter Five

## *Aftershock*

It was around then that the *Aftershock* column in the *Sunday Times* was born. I had to make some money to pay the bills while I considered the big 'What do you want?' question. I reckoned writing the column might give me about a day's work a month, which wasn't going to make me rich, or even keep me from starving – but it would be a start. And, more importantly, it would put me in touch with other people who were in the same position as I was. I'd worked in journalism all my life, and everyone had always told me that the important thing was to write about what you know. Well, what I knew most intimately just then was redundancy – perhaps I would pick up some ideas, make some contacts. And anyway, what did I have to lose? I emailed someone on the paper I had known from years before.

## THE CALLER FROM HELL

When he didn't reply, I emailed again. And when he didn't reply to the second email, I phoned him. He wasn't in, of course, so I phoned him again. And again – and eventually, we spoke. He'd read the email, he said, and he liked the idea of a column, but he'd have to run it past his editor, so he'd get back to me later.

And later. And later. So after about a month, I called again, desperately sounding as cheery as I could. 'I was just wondering ...' Oh yes, there wasn't a problem, it was just that moving the idea forward was taking a bit more time than he'd expected, so I'd have to wait a little longer.

Perhaps I could send him a sample of the column I was thinking of writing? So, my heart leaping, I sat down and wrote a thousand words about being made redundant, and sent it off to him. From about an hour after I had sent it, I started checking my inbox to see if I'd had a reply. I hadn't.

Another month passed, and I rang again. And again. And again. Sometimes I spoke to him, sometimes to his secretary – she actually became quite conspiratorial with me, advising me on the best times to ambush him in his office – but whichever one of them I caught, I began to imagine the long-suffering way in which their eyes must be rolling to the ceiling as I said 'Hi, it's Andrew Taylor here . . .'; the way their knuckles must be whitening as they gripped the phone, and the stratagems they must be devising to shake this relentlessly upbeat parasite out of their lives. I had read, as everyone has, the stories of famous writers who, in their early days, had received enough rejection slips to paper their walls with – but I wasn't even getting as far as the rejection slips. So I kept on phoning. Needy? Clingy? It must have seemed in the *Sunday Times* office that I grew out of their telephone like poison ivy. I wrapped my tendrils around their necks. They must have woken up in the night, screaming with nightmares about that obscenely reasonable, relentless voice. If there were any justice, I would have been locked up for causing mental suffering to innocent people. I had become a telephone pest, a stalker, the caller from hell – and so, like all the creepiest characters in those late-night television movies, I became as friendly and as casual and as agreeable as

I knew how – *Desperate Housewives* meets *The Boston Strangler*. If I was poison ivy, I was going to be poison ivy with flowers and a cheery voice. And I kept calling.

That was the first lesson that I learned – the important thing is just to keep in there, smiling as hard as you can, not admitting even to yourself that you're beginning to think the whole enterprise is a waste of time. Why would you get bad tempered? After all, the man I was emailing, I have absolutely no doubt at all, was doing his best for me. What was there to achieve by being grumpy with him when I called yet again, other than giving him an excuse that he could use to himself to tell me to go to hell and slam the phone down for the final time?

## THE *AFTERSHOCK* GENERATION

The second lesson I learned, once the first *Aftershock* column actually appeared in the paper, was that there was virtually no limit to the different answers people had to my 'What do you want?' question. I had hundreds of emails from people who had been through just the same experience that I had. Many of them had ended up working for themselves – self-employment has all the obvious benefits of autonomy, such as making your own decisions and drawing up your own timetables, and possibly working from home. Others were working as volunteers for good causes or charities, rather than planning out a career simply for money. They may not have planned to take on 'portfolio careers' by filling their weeks with several activities rather than a single job, but it had often crept up on them quietly, when they weren't looking.

There were disillusioned professionals who had retrained as tradesmen and skilled workers – boardroom whiz-kids who were now driving round as plumbers, or accountants who had turned themselves into go-any-where, do-anything handymen. There were some of the most unlikely career changes, by people who had thought laterally about what they could do and what they had done, and how those might chime in with what they would like to do.

Women, maybe because many of them had started their working lives with at least the possibility at the back of their minds that they might take a break or change di-rection at some time before retirement, seemed to be better at taking stock and mapping out a new life than men. Joyce wrote that she had been sacked when the charity for which she worked reorganised her job out of existence – and at 56, and a self-confessed computer-illiterate, her prospects didn't seem good. Earlier in her career, though, she had trained and worked as a nurse; she didn't want to go back to that, but she wondered how she might put the experience to good use. And what exactly *was* that experience, anyway? She had literally leafed through the Yellow Pages looking for inspiration – anything that might spark an idea for a new career. And when she got towards the end of the F's, she paused. Her time as a nurse had never been only a matter of med-ical knowledge and skill; what her nursing background had given her too was subtlety and sensitivity in dealing with people when they were sick, suffering, and in pain and grief.

A thought had struck her. She had never, ever heard of a woman funeral director. It's not an occupation that most people would think of as a barrel of fun every day – but her own years on the hospital wards had taught her that dealing with people in the extremes of grief didn't have to be maudlin or depressing. It could be uplifting and rewarding – and she knew that she could do it. Was the fact that women didn't seem to work in the industry a draw-back? After all, the law may say that it is illegal to refuse to employ a woman just because she *is* a woman, although any woman knows there are hundreds of ways to get round that one. Or was the dearth of female funeral directors, just possibly, an opportunity? There was only one way to find out. Like me, she was ready to write hundreds of letters and make hundreds of calls if she had to – but unlike me, she didn't have to.

Just about the first letter she wrote brought a reply from the intrigued owner of a company of funeral directors. Would she come and see him? When they met he was cautious – no doubt thinking about the Equal Opportunity legislation – but fascinated. She had no experience in the industry, he noted – and he'd never actually *had* an application from a woman before. And then she played her trump card – had it occurred to him, she asked, that some clients might *prefer* to deal with a woman? That by having her on his staff, he might give his own firm a bit of an advantage in the cut-throat world of bless, burn and bury (my disrespectful phrase, not hers)?

He was impressed not just because she was so pro-active, but because she had spotted a gap in the market that nobody else seemed to have noticed, and he gave her a trial. It was the start of a very successful career as the first woman funeral director in the south-west of England. 'I think imagination, an open mind and a "What have I got to lose?" attitude can sometimes be more important than skills,' she said.

Another woman, Anna, had recently walked out on a 20-year teaching career to try her luck in what she cheerfully admitted was the most ageist world of them all – the music industry. She had formed a band with her husband, they had brought out a CD, and kept themselves busy playing gigs all over Scotland. 'This is what I always wanted to do, but my career and my children always took priority,' she said. 'If we are all being forced to work till we drop, it had better be something we enjoy. I'm in control of my life now, so I can do supply teaching when it's available, and at other times I can write, perform and record songs.'

Another correspondent was in the process of setting up a small film production company, another one working as a French polisher. Some had healthy redundancy payments to keep them comfortable, some had been laid off with the bare minimum that their employers could get away with, and others had bitten the bullet themselves and simply set out on their own. I guess you need to be an accountant to work out whether that is a good idea – one of my messages *was* from an accountant who was working as a gardener – and I bet that when they do the sums and work out the effect on your pension, your financial advisers will tell you it's about as close to madness as you can get without being put into a straitjacket. But *no-one cared!*

Many of the emails were from people in their forties and fifties, and there were a few bitter tirades about unfeeling employers, employment agencies who weren't interested in anyone too old to have acne, and companies who thought that anyone who remembered the 1970s was only fit for a wheelchair and slippers – but the overwhelming feeling was one of optimism. This was the *Aftershock* generation – there was a life out there, and these people were determined to take it. But there was one other thought that came through time and again – that however the sums added up, whatever the financially sensible thing was to do, the one certainty was that this week, this month, this year weren't going to come again. The best thing to do was to fill them with the things you enjoy doing.

I've never quite understood why people write to newspapers, unless they want their thoughts to be published on the 'Letters' page. These people weren't writing because they wanted their names in the paper, but just to let me know what their experiences had been, as if I were a friend or at least someone they had met, rather than just the name at the top of an article – but I certainly hope that writing their experiences down made them feel better, because reading what they had written did wonders for me. If all these people could find this huge variety of ways to start a new life, then surely I could do the same. I'd had a similar sort of feeling years before, when I started a course of chemotherapy at the cancer clinic. When I'd first walked in, and seen all those strange-looking people, many with no hair, and most looking painfully thin, it seemed as if I was walking into a club that I had no interest in joining – but once I'd met a few of them, and sat down and talked with them, I changed my mind. If they could be so defiant, upbeat and determined, then so could I.

And anyway, just like in the cancer clinic, I had no choice. The one option that nobody had mentioned in all the emails was doing nothing.

That's not to say, of course, that the do-nothing option doesn't exist. I know several people who have had more or less generous pay-offs, and simply decided that they want to stop working. At anything. They imagine that life is simply going to be a well-cushioned and stress-free round of holidays, golf, television, and gardening – which I guess it might be, given the money. And on the face of it, perhaps it sounds a pretty attractive way to spend your time. But it never seems to work out like that, because most people seem to need a purpose in their lives. One of the emails I got came from Geoff, the former managing director of a Midlands engineering business who had lost his job when the company was taken over. He had applied for several promising-looking jobs without even getting an interview, and then he made up his mind that he had simply to get himself into some kind of employment. 'I took several temporary jobs – driving, mainly, and paying around £5 an hour, but at least it got me out of the house and off the dole queue. After a few months of delivering fat to fish and chip shops, I felt as fit as a butcher's dog, and ready for a new challenge,' he wrote.

In his spare time from driving the van, he had been negotiating to put the money he had taken with him from his old company into a new business that the owner was trying to sell – and within a few years, he was back in control of his own destiny again. It may not be paid employment that they look for – we'll look later, for instance, at the choice many people make of volunteering for various forms of charity work – but most people, even if they don't have the money or the talents to buy themselves a company, need to do *something*.

As for the ones who don't – well, we all end up dead in the end, but I have a sneaking feeling that they get there a lot sooner than the rest of us.

## DOING NOTHING

But that too, of course, is a choice that some people make. In August 1985, Ken Baldwin jumped off the Golden Gate Bridge in San Francisco. He was 28 years old, and he had been suffering from depression for more than two years. Since the bridge is 225 feet above the surging currents of the Pacific Ocean, and since 98 per cent of the people who jump off it die, it's fairly sure that he wasn't looking for a new life – but that's what he found. Miraculously, he survived the fall, and now, cured of his depression and working as a high school teacher, he mentally divides his life into 'Before the jump' and 'After the jump'. He reckons he is lucky to be alive, and he relishes every day.

Fourteen years later and on the other side of the Atlantic, my experience was similar, though much less dramatic. In much the same way as Ken Baldwin thinks back over his past, I now think about life before I heard the doctor tell me about the cancer which might well kill me, and life afterwards – and there is no doubt which has been more satisfying.

I'm not saying that cancer is a way to a more fulfilling life, and I'm certainly not stupid enough to recommend jumping off the Golden Gate Bridge as a means of curing depression – but what I am suggesting is that a disaster in your life can prove to be a turning point. The first proviso, of course, is that the disaster has to be matched by a lucky break – if Ken Baldwin had simply been swept out to sea and the sharks, or if I hadn't got better, neither of us would have been celebrating the turnaround in our lives – but the good thing about redundancy is that it offers the turning point without the possibility of actually killing you.

Among the letters and emails that came in to the *Aftershock* column were the angry ones, the bitter ones, the dispirited ones and the defiant ones – but what was remarkable was the number of people who wrote that, once they had got over the initial shock, redundancy had proved to be a truly positive experience. It had, one of them said, kick-started his life when it seemed to be running down. I know from my own experience that, as you contemplate life outside the comfort zone of the office chair and the monthly cheque, that might seem to be an almost offensively Pollyanna-ish and head-in-the-clouds thought – 'You can talk about opportunities all you want, mate, but

I have three kids to support and a mortgage to pay!' as one good friend said to me, when he thought I hadn't quite realised what had hit him. But the evidence of all those letters and emails is that, for many people, being kicked out of a job was, in the end, like being kicked out of a prison they had barely known they were in. There is a life outside.

**NOTES**

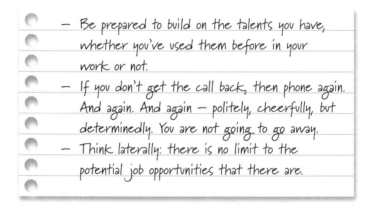

— Be prepared to build on the talents you have, whether you've used them before in your work or not.

— If you don't get the call back, then phone again. And again. And again — politely, cheerfully, but determinedly. You are not going to go away.

— Think laterally: there is no limit to the potential job opportunities that there are.

# Chapter Six

## Grabbing at Logs

**T**he *Aftershock* column was a lot of fun, and it brought me lots of ideas for new ways to deal with redundancy and new paths to follow, but I still had to find a way of earning money to live on – and I still had to find that new life which I was convinced was hiding somewhere. As we've seen, a lot of people who are made redundant want to get back into what they were doing before as fast as they can and try and forget the whole embarrassing and unsettling experience of being thrown out on their ear. There's nothing wrong with that – but others want to do something new, different, and maybe more challenging. Some come to that realisation almost instinctively, as soon as they realise that they're on their own, while for others, it takes a few rejection letters and a couple of unsuccessful interviews. It is, as one *Aftershock* correspondent wrote to me, 'the grey revolution of the unwanted-but-doing-quite-nicely-thank-you' – or at least, it becomes that once you have found your way to that something new. Finding what that something might be demands patience and confidence – patience to keep swimming, and confidence not to grab the first log that comes floating past.

## UNAVAILABLE, UNSUITABLE, OR SIMPLY POTTY ...
## LOOKING FOR JOBS

I certainly grabbed at a few entirely unsuitable logs in those first panicky weeks, although none so obviously barmy as the brief moment when I looked at a poster advertising for new firemen and thought, 'Yes, I could do that.' Everything seemed to stack up – a worthwhile job, reasonable pay, working with other people, and a complete change from anything I had done before. My new life lay mapped out in front of me for about two seconds, which was as long as it took me to realise that I was a good 20 years above the age limit on the advertisement, and correspondingly overweight and out of condition. And in any case, one of my ideas of perfect hell would be swaying about at the top of a turntable ladder with the whole world mapped out beneath me in hideous clarity.

All in all, I think I had more rejections over those first few weeks than I'd had since I was a gangly youth with spots and high ambitions in the discos of Huddersfield 40 years ago. More realistic than the ambition to roll back the years and turn myself into Fireman Sam – though not much – was the possibility of a part-time role back in a television company, doing much the same sort of job as I had slouched unwillingly to work at for several years before I got my fax. That was a hopelessly wrong choice for a whole load of different reasons, and I look back at it now and shiver with horror at the thought that I might actually have got the job. Television is a bit like working a puppet show – it never feels quite the same once you have seen the ramshackle way it works behind the scenes. It's a young person's business, and luckily, they thought so too. A young man in a sharp suit with a mid-Atlantic voice, who squeezed slightly too many words into each sentence and too many teeth into each smile, oozed caring sympathy as he helped put my coat on and look for my bus pass after our chat in his office. Well, I *was* a couple of years over 50, so perhaps he was simply being polite when he seemed to lean forward a touch and raise his voice slightly for my benefit as he promised he would get in touch. He didn't.

Then there was the bijou independent little *chocolatier*, which was looking for someone to train to make chocolates and then sell them. *That*, I thought, is the job for me! And what could be more worthwhile, what could bring more happiness into the world at large and mine in particular, than producing trays of glistening brown chocolate? Admittedly it paid slightly less than a teenage hoody on work experience would expect to get for wiping tables in a coffee bar, and I had no remotely relevant experience, along with the manual dexterity of a drunken gorilla – but the prospect of spending my days up to my wrists in molten chocolate, only pausing occasionally to lick my fingers clean before plunging them back into the delicious warm goo, was just too good to resist. I rang the number on the advertisement, full of hope and enthusiasm. After all, how would it be possible to resist an application from a man of my years and gravitas? Well, suffice to say that it was. Possibly the fact that I admitted that I found chocolates irresistible had something to do with it – for some reason, the owner of the shop seemed to have a prejudice against people who might eat the value of their own wages during a quiet morning shift without even noticing it. Whatever the reason, I never heard back from him either, and was thus spared the prospect of rotten teeth within five years, a 55-inch waistline within five months, and the chance to work long hours for not very much money.

And there was the driving job, which would have meant me finding my way around the streets of London with high-powered executives in the back of the car – an interesting option for a man who can get lost going from one end of a train to the other. And one job in a library, and another which would have involved me in helping a friend look after her clients' gardens – me, who only has to look at a plant to kill it, and for whom spending time in a garden is slightly less appealing than hammering six-inch nails into my own feet with a sledgehammer. At times it felt as if I was living that old cherry-stones rhyme – tinker, tailor, soldier, sailor. And of course, there was the day with a plumber.

It is a well-known fact among people who wear a tie and go to dinner parties that plumbers earn squillions of pounds an hour, and drive around in Rolls Royces when they are not intimidating other road users by driving much too close to them in the beaten-up white vans which they use for camouflage. What could make more sense than to get myself qualified and join their number? It was a practical proposition, after all: I got the idea from an email from a former executive called John, who was committing £8,000 of his savings and his redundancy payment to getting trained and qualified at the age of 49, after a career as an audit manager. The classes he was going to were split about 50/50 between school-leavers and people of his own age. He had no illusions about the pay – £25,000 a year was roughly what he was hoping to make eventually from working for a big company, though he could always boost that by doing a bit on his own account on the side – and, even if that is not exactly squillions, he reckoned that in three or four years' time, he would have a new set of skills and a job that he would enjoy and that he could keep doing for as long as he liked.

One big advantage I had to start with was that I have a friend called Vince, who runs a successful plumbing business of his own, and who was happy to take me out with him for the day, as long as I earned my keep. The trouble was, from my point of view, that I have always been to DIY what Tommy Cooper was to the Magic Circle. Hammering in a nail without bending it is a personal triumph of manual dexterity and hand-to-eye co-ordination. It's enough to say that my day as a plumber's mate was a very valuable learning experience, if only in the sense that I found out, as I squatted on my hands and knees under a sink, tightening a perfect stranger's taps while the pipes dripped cold water down my arms, that there was one more thing that I couldn't do.

As I got out of the van at the end of the day, Vince stopped me. 'If you ever think of taking up plumbing . . .' he said, and my heart leapt. He was going to offer to take me on. I must have shown skills that I didn't know I had, even when I'd managed to soak him. There is no Andrex puppy as pathetic as a man who's told he's good at something he never dreamed he could manage.

'If you ever think of taking up plumbing,' Vince repeated, slowly and clearly, 'you'll starve'. And he grinned. I guess he was right.

## THANKS, BUT NO THANKS ...

Half the time, I suspect I didn't really want the jobs at all.
(Well, I have to believe that. The alternative explanation for
my selecting such an unsuitable assortment of potential
roles is that I was barking mad – which is, I have to accept, another possibility.) It was brought home to me when I
finally received an email from a company I had approached
several weeks before. I had applied soon after I lost my
job – or rather, soon after my job lost me – for a job in PR. I
forgot all about the application, as you do, and they didn't
bother to reply, as they don't – one of the lessons most
people learn once they have been made redundant is that
those nice, friendly Human Resources types who are so
outgoing and positive when they speak to you actually answer about one application in five hundred – and then one
day, a message popped up in my inbox from the company.
In fact, they'd decided that they didn't want me either, but
that wasn't the important thing. What was significant was
my reaction when I first saw the message and who it was
from. Before I even opened it, I looked at the address and
thought, 'Oh no!' Pictures of the early morning slog down
the motorway, the seat in the office, the miserable churn-
ing out of stuff I didn't believe in for people who didn't care
about it, all floated in front of my eyes, and my immediate
reaction when I read their 'Thanks but no thanks' was one
of immense relief.

After a while, I got to enjoy it. There was, in fact, something exciting, if not entirely convincing, about the feeling
that there were infinite possibilities stretching out in front

of me. Then there was another thought: I come from a family of teachers – my schoolmaster father, when I first went into journalism, wondered genially when I was going to get a proper job, by which I assumed he meant something in a school – so that seemed like a realistic option. After all, the Government was always banging on about the need to get people with experience back into teaching, and offering tax-free training bursaries of between £5,000 and £6,000: there would presumably be no problems there about being too old in my fifties. Teaching, after all, actively seeks out older applicants – and it's getting them. About a third of new secondary school teachers who come into the profession late have previously held senior management jobs, and something like 12 per cent of teachers are over 40 years old. So I spoke to a friend who ran an agency supplying temporary teachers to schools in the north of England.

'No problem,' he said; he could fit me in as a teacher's assistant, and I would be able to have a look at what schools were like now. At £10 an hour or so, that was never going to make me rich, but it did seem like a good way to take a peep over the edge of the frying pan before leaping into the fire. Well, 'no problem' turned out to be a bit of an exaggeration: before I could even think about walking into a school, I had to have a whole series of official checks to see if I had a criminal record. That was easy enough, as I've never actually been caught doing anything wrong – but it took several weeks. Teaching isn't a spur of the moment decision, then.

But I had no qualms about being able to cope. Teaching is one of those jobs we all think we can do: after all, we've all been to school, haven't we? And I don't remember ever thinking as a teenager that my teachers were having such a tough time. But then I went into my first class. All I had to do was help the teacher – just sit with the pupils and help to explain the lessons as they went ahead – but for the first half-hour, I could only watch in amazement. I suppose I should have realised – although few of us do – that things had changed a bit in 40 years.

It wasn't an easy school that I had been placed in – the staff had spent the previous two years turning it round from an 'unsatisfactory' rating to 'good', after five years in special measures – the Department for Education and Skills equivalent of extra lessons after class for poor perfor-mance. But inside the classroom, it was like a high-energy non-stop stage show, a mixture of the old *Sunday Night at the London Palladium*, the *Big Brother* house and top-flight stand-up comedy – a bit like watching Jimmy Carr or Eddie Izzard on speed. The teacher I was supposed to be shadowing had come into the profession in his late twenties after a short career in the civil service, and I don't think he'd sat down since. He just never stopped. There was banter, joking, one-liners, and a very occasional hard stare as he kept the children amused, but busy as well. Twenty minutes of it would have left me wiped out for the day, but no sooner had the first lesson ended than the second performance began.

This time, I did manage to offer a bit of nervous assis-tance to the boy I'd been assigned to, although I'm still not sure how much either of us really understood about what the other was saying. I rather gathered that I lacked that indefinable air of magisterial authority when he offered me a surreptitious piece of chewing gum. As a classroom assistant, of course, I wasn't supposed to keep anyone in order, but if I wanted to be a teacher, I would need not only a proper teaching qualification – a one-year course for a graduate – but also a flair that is a combination of acting, listening, understanding, and refusing to be thrown off your stride.

It's certainly worthwhile in all sorts of ways – the payback of having some stranger come up to greet you in the street, and gradually recognising the outlines of a face you last saw looking at you from behind a desk, is one of the things that hasn't changed. All the teachers I spoke to said that knowing they had made a difference to the children they taught was what made the job worth doing, and I remember my father saying much the same thing 30 years or so ago.

But could I do it? Well, there certainly are late entrants to the profession who make a big success of it – the head at the school I was at suggested sceptically that they tend to be either brilliant or hopeless, but not often anywhere in between – but it's not a job that is for everyone. If you're passionate about it, and if you have the talent, then I suspect it is one of a very few ways to spend your life that are wholly worthwhile and wholly honourable. There is no doubt about the rewards – even after my shaky hour in class, the moment when the boy I'd been sitting with sidled up to me, glanced round to see that none of his mates were watching, and then said 'Thanks for the help,' was as big a buzz as I had got out of any sort of work for a very long time.

But it's time to be honest with yourself, I thought. If you're not instinctively enthused by the idea of teaching children, or if you are daft enough to think it is some sort of soft option with long holidays, then you would be better off finding something easier and less stressful. Something like taming lions, fighting sharks, or tickling piranhas.

So no, teaching wasn't the answer to my problem. In fact, at that depressing stage of the game, nothing much seemed to be. What I still wanted, for all my public bravado, was for someone to offer me *something*. I had got over the fist-shaking anger, and I was deep in the terror of thinking that no-one was ever going to offer me a job at all. Like most people, I hadn't thought initially that I would be out of work for long, but that early confidence had rapidly ebbed away. Maybe I had been wrong to treat those offers of professional help from the agency with such contempt – although, rightly or wrongly, I felt there was no going back in that direction. I still needed to sort out a strategy to answer the question of what I wanted, and to work out a way to get it.

## NOTES

- Look for some sticking-plaster jobs while you work out what you really want to do – they're good for your pride, good for your CV, and good for your bank balance.
- Be honest with yourself about what enthuses you.
- Check out the internet – apart from anything else, it's a good reminder of how many people are in the same position as you.

# Chapter Seven

## Becoming Gordon Ramsay

There were all sorts of lessons that I learned in those first frantic months after I was made redundant. But by far the most important ones were how to iron a shirt and how to make a fish pie.

Perhaps it's a slight exaggeration to say that I was completely incapable of both things before – but only in the sense that, like most men of my age, I had always been able to wave a hot iron around in the general vicinity of a newly washed shirt and render it vaguely wearable. And I suppose anyone can throw a few pieces of fish into a dish and then hide them under a layer of mashed potato. But within a few weeks of leaving my job, though I say it myself, my ironing would not have disgraced the laundry room at the Ritz, and my fish pies were so good that even Gordon Ramsay wouldn't have been able to find fault with them. (If he had tried, he might have learned some useful additions to his vocabulary of obscenity and invective, but that's a different story. The secret, by the way, is a few shallots and a lot of white wine.)

## A SENSIBLE INVESTMENT

It's not that I ever thought of starting a laundry to make a living, or still less – no doubt to Gordon Ramsay's great relief – of opening a fish restaurant. But I am in no doubt about the importance of these accomplishments – certainly greater than finding my way around the benefit system, brushing up my techniques on the computer, or developing a salesman's patter and networking skills.

On one level, it's simply a question of strategy and intelligent self-interest. If you are made redundant and you are lucky enough to have a partner at home to support you – and that word *support* can mean anything from bringing in an income to offering you occasional reassurance that you are not chronically unemployable, morally reprehensible and personally repulsive – then the best effort of time and money that you can make is in keeping them happy. And in my limited experience, I can think of few better ways to do that than with a steaming hot fish pie at the end of the day, preferably served with a large glass of chilled white wine, and to a background of half a dozen freshly ironed shirts hanging by the wall. A cynic might add that if your partner is going out to work, as mine was, then an important trick is always to start your own work at least 20 minutes before she gets home, to lend verisimilitude to your claim to have spent the entire day – except for the time invested in the fish pie and the ironing – sweating over a hot keyboard.

All right, so I'm joking – sort of. But the fact remains that it's a big bonus to have a partner who *is* earning some money while you are struggling to sort out your next move, and who doesn't make you feel that you're not pulling your weight. I had, and I knew how lucky I was, so having dinner ready when she got home seemed to be the best thing to do. The money from *one* wage-earner in the house is obviously a big comfort for both of you: it may push away the day when you'll need to sell up and start busking. But even if your other half isn't working either, you're still going to need some help and support. Personal crises – all sorts of crises – can either drive couples apart or bring them closer together, so it's worth working out the best ways to see that they do the latter.

## PLAYING TO THE GALLERY

And there's another benefit to having someone else around: there's an audience to encourage you to put on a bit of an act. I'm not suggesting that you should be dishonest, or at least not more so than most of us are most of the time, and I'm certainly not in favour of bottling up the way you are really feeling – but putting on an occasional show of confidence, of defiance, or of simple, straightforward happiness, can be a very effective way of keeping yourself from getting depressed and negative. It's a lesson I learned in hospital, when people came in to see me, and I struggled as hard as I could to seem cheerful and upbeat. If you talk loudly enough, and smile for your visitors while you are crumbling inside, then you can fool yourself as well as the people around you, and suddenly find that you really do feel as confident as you are pretending. Sometimes when the visitors leave, you'll collapse in weariness and despair – but at others, if you've acted the part hard enough, then the pretence begins to turn into a sort of reality of its own. The same thing works when you're out of bed and simply mooching around the house, wondering how on earth you are going to find a job.

None of this is easy on either side. If you've just lost your job, you're likely to be feeling raw and vulnerable, and it can be tempting to be defensive and scratchy with the people about you. I suspect, looking back, that I was often as cuddly as a sheet of coarse-grained sandpaper. Of course, it's important to keep those feelings in check – but you also have to realise the limits of what you can hope for from your other half. Sympathy, yes. Support, yes, and someone to chew over ideas with. But a realistic appraisal of your talents and abilities? Hard-hitting advice that you may find uncomfortable but, on reflection, will decide is probably right? A reality check when your ideas really seem to be flying? If these are what you want, then the person who is closest to you, like your friends but even more so, is probably not the right one to turn to. The very fact that they are non-negotiably on your side means that their view is likely to be biased. Comforting, perhaps, but not necessarily helpful in the end.

And if you *are* the other half – if you're dealing with someone who has just lost their job – well, the best way of putting it that I heard was from an old friend whose husband had just parted company – very acrimoniously – with his employers. She said that it was like living with an adolescent all over again. It felt as if all the floors in their house were covered with eggshells, over which she had to pick her way with infinite care, knowing that one false step, one wrong remark, could cause a disaster.

On the one hand, she needed to show that she was there and supportive, and demonstrate that she was interested in the efforts to find a new direction, and confident that they would be successful – but on the other hand, it was important to avoid asking questions all the time as if she didn't believe in what was going on. Yes, she wanted to be honest and to give good advice, but at the same time,

she needed to inject a little icy realism into the more out-
landish schemes that she was hearing. Think of how you
would fix props to buttress a brick wall, with their feet set
in the ground a good few feet from the wall itself, she said:
sometimes the best way to offer support can be from a distance. Anyway, her answer was to keep in touch with how
his search for a new role was going by listening carefully
when he told their friends. It was just simpler that way.

Children come into the picture too, as they tend to. One
of the commonest feelings I found among the men I spoke
to who had lost their jobs was the sense that they had
somehow let their children down. We may gush about how
wonderful it is to spend more time with the family – we
may, unlike the sacked politicians who parrot the phrase
through gritted teeth as they leave office, even mean it –
but deep, deep inside, in even the newest new man, lurks
the primeval feeling that he should be the hunter-gatherer,
the provider, the one who leaves the cave each day to track
down the woolly mammoth for supper. We want to be role
models for our children, and we have an uneasy feeling that
this involves something more than cooking supper and lying on the sofa watching endless reruns of *The Guns of
Navarone* on daytime television – after all, in my experience, most children need no instruction at all in how to lie
comatose in front of the television screen.

And of course, it's no longer just a male problem.
Women have their own hang-ups too – by 'failing' in
the employment market-place, they are sending out all
the wrong signals about a woman's role. By staying at
home because they haven't got a job, they are reinforcing

the stereotype of the stay-at-home wife and mother and probably doing lasting damage to their children as well. That's the way it feels, anyway, several people told me. In their heads, they might know it was all baloney, but in their hearts, they hurt like hell.

It is all unnecessary angst, just another way of beating yourself up. Most children, at least until they are teenagers, have no real idea what their parents do anyway. One good friend who had a very high-powered job shuffling money around from one file to another in a City bank explained to his three-year-old daughter that he had to go off to work each day to get some money. He was horrified, some time later, to find that her mental picture of his day at work involved him standing in front of an automatic cash machine, repeatedly putting his cash card in and taking out the notes that presented themselves so politely to him. That, she knew, was what happened when Daddy stopped the car to get some money – that, clearly, was what he did when he went off to the office each day. She wasn't so far wrong, either.

By the time they've grown out of ideas like that and reached the magic teenage years of spots, hair-trigger tempers and butterfly-like attention spans, all they know is that whatever it is their parents do at work, it is certainly something sad, pathetic, and inescapably embarrassing; and after that – well, they are in the job market themselves, and far too busy paddling their own canoes to worry too much about them.

When my marriage was falling apart, I went through all the same fears that anyone in the same position will go through: how would it affect my relationship with my children? ('Have you thought of the children?' someone asked me helpfully. Had I thought about the children? Had I remembered to breathe? Had I thought about anything else as I lay awake at night?) A slightly more perceptive friend told me the reassuring truth that unless you do something drastic to change their point of view, children love their mum and they love their dad. Simple as that. Given their choices, they would probably prefer to love them together and in one house – but if they can't do that, then they generally want them to be happy wherever they are living. If that's true for divorce, how much simpler and more true it is when all that is involved is a job. Far from being part of the problem, they are part of the solution. They're on your side.

And anyway, the older I get, the more convinced I am that trying to protect your children is generally a waste of time. They are tougher than you think, and they certainly know much more than you suppose. When I was ill, I lay in my hospital bed torturing myself for hours at a time with the need to keep from my children the disagreeable fact that there was a significant chance that their father would not be walking out of this hospital ward – probably not soon, and quite possibly not ever. When they came to see me, I would gee myself up into a ghastly sort of cheery optimism – they were the most important audience of all the people who came to visit me and see this particular cabaret – and quite frequently, I would fall apart after they left. Of course, as I've mentioned before, there were benefits to me in all this play-acting, because the faked optimism gradually turned into real optimism, and pretending to feel good became the real thing – but the point is that I didn't want my children, then aged between ten and 16, to know exactly how serious things were. And I thought I had done a pretty good job.

And then, out of hospital a few months later, I was looking through an album of old family photographs with my youngest daughter, who was now 11 years old. There was a picture there of me as a small boy, standing with my sister. It was she who had given me the bone marrow transplant that had kept me alive. My daughter looked at it, and said brightly: 'How odd to think that little girl never knew that one day she would save your life.' She'd known all along, as I should have guessed she would. Who had been looking after whom?

Losing your job is in a different league from nearly losing your life, but they both open your eyes. One of the ironies of using hoary old clichés like the one I mentioned earlier in connection with redundancy is the fact that many of them turn out, despite themselves, to be absolutely true – 'more time with your family' is potentially one of the big bonuses of losing your job, not part of the . . . downside. I heard a story of one man who, six or seven weeks into the long grind of application forms, situations vacant columns and unanswered letters, was putting his six-year-old son to bed one night. 'I'd been honest with him right from the start, and told him that I'd lost my job,' he said. 'He didn't seem to have taken it in – certainly, he'd never said anything about it.'

And then, that night, he did. 'He looked up at me and rolled his eyes up in his head,' he said. 'It was as if he was completely exasperated. "Are you *ever* going to get another job?" he asked, and I felt as if he'd hit me. It was the sort of tone of voice I used to use if I asked if he was ever going to tidy his bedroom.' So the father mumbled something back about trying his best, and being sure that it wouldn't be long before he was back at work, and wanting to find a really good job – but the little boy wasn't listening.

'I hope you don't,' he said wistfully. 'It's much, much nicer like this.'

## SO WHO IS CENTRE STAGE?

Whether the crisis is redundancy, sickness, bereavement or even death, I suspect – though I have no direct personal experience of that so far, and don't expect to be writing books about it when I have – it can be a great deal easier to go through for the person at the centre of it than it is for the people on the edge, who love and care for him or her. Certainly, being made redundant is a challenge not just for the person who opens the letter with the P45 form enclosed, but for everyone around as well. They need looking after too.

We all work out our own ways of dealing with the problems for ourselves – and if we look for them, we will also find the benefits of this new way of living. Janice, who lived in Richmond, Surrey, wrote to Aftershock to say that both she and her husband had been made redundant by different employers within about six weeks of each other – obviously, I thought, the start of another painful story of cruel bad luck. There were more than enough of those. But not a bit of it. 'We're just discovering again how well we get on together,' she said. 'For the last few years, we've both been concentrating on our careers, and without realising it, I don't think we were taking as much notice of each other as we used to. Now we do stuff together again – just simple things, like the shopping, or going out to a pub on the spur of the moment in the middle of the day, and it's fantastic.'

'We're going to have to sort out new jobs eventually, or maybe we'll start some kind of business that we can work at as a couple – but right now, we're just enjoying the time together.'

Not every disaster, of course, has a fairy-tale ending. But the chance to sit down together and reassess your life can't be a bad thing. And, once you get the white wine and the shallots sorted, the freshly cooked fish pie at the end of the day makes up for a great deal.

## NOTES

— If you're lucky enough to have a partner, bring
him or her on board — but don't look to them
for a realistic view of your talents, your skills,
or your ideas.
— Never underestimate how important it is to
put on an act.
— Most of all — learn how to make a fish pie,
or something!

# Chapter Eight

## Selling Yourself

didn't want to waste my time – that, perhaps, was another legacy of the cancer from all those years ago. I had to be realistic – at 52, it was a bit late to be starting off in some entirely new direction if that meant training and qualifications. Not only was I never going to run the 1500 metres in the Olympics, I wasn't going to become a doctor either; I might follow the example of one good friend and start a university course, but if I was thinking of investing three or four years in acquiring the training and knowledge for a completely new career, there would be some pretty daunting hurdles in my way. A few people might do it, but then a few people climb Everest as well. So although I might want to learn new skills – in fact, I definitely *did* want to learn new skills – I also wanted to use the ones I had developed so far in my life. That, in fact, seemed to be the key not just to earning the money that I needed with the least possible disruption to my life, but also to laying the foundations for a rewarding and enjoyable few years.

I sensed that I was feeling my way uncertainly towards a sensible solution, without really having any idea what it was – but while I was getting there, I still kept on sticking in applications for all sorts of jobs. There, on reflection, was another lesson – that most of us can manage to keep two completely contradictory thoughts in our heads at the same time. As I was making my mind up that I didn't want to work for anyone again, I was busily sending off applications to do just that. And not only that – I was putting myself through the misery of attending the interviews that people offered me.

## SOMEONE I ONCE KNEW ...

I dimly remembered a fresh-faced young boy with a constant smile that I seemed once to have known vaguely. He seemed like a visitor from another planet now, with his slightly ill-fitting and obviously new suit, his eager attentiveness and his irritating desire to please – someone, I thought, should tell him not to say so enthusiastically that absolutely everything is 'exciting' and 'a real challenge'. But there was something worryingly familiar about him too, particularly as I looked at the slightly battered but still recognisable face that stared back at me from the shaving mirror each morning. Was that really the me of 30 years ago?

In fact, I don't feel that ashamed of him. Don't we all have times we'd rather forget, like first dates, early disasters with alcohol, and those flared trousers and massive lapels we thought looked so trendy back in the 70s? And interviews – especially interviews. However ruthlessly we try to slap him away, the person we once were keeps on coming back to haunt us.

Probably the least useful thing I ever did in my life – and there is considerable competition for that title – was going on a course that promised to turn me into a super-salesman. (In fact, now I come to think about it, it was so long ago that it was actually that fresh-faced, smiling young boy who turned up on the course rather than me, which makes me feel a little better about it.) With that grotesque, unreasonable, and entirely random optimism that you have in your twenties, I pictured myself jetting around the world clinching multi-million pound oil deals, signing contracts for whole fleets of battleships, or haggling over the final £5 million on a docklands office block. Beautiful women would look dreamily at the finely cut diamonds nestling in the palm of my hand, or dark-eyed Arab potentates would run a hand lightly down the flank of the most expensive racehorse in the world, which I was offering to sell them. It didn't matter what it was I was going to sell, there would be sackloads of profit in it for me.

My fellow students, I suspect, are still out there somewhere, flogging draughty double glazing or cold-calling harassed housewives to inquire about their life insurance – but the instructor took me on one side after a couple of lessons. 'Andrew,' he said – and he was a patient man – 'you couldn't sell ice-packs in the desert. You couldn't persuade a drowning man to buy a lifebelt. You are to selling what Macbeth was to the Scottish bed and breakfast industry. Do yourself a favour, mate, and try something else. Now.'

I gathered from this that he believed that, on balance, my talents might be better employed in a different field, but I've never forgotten one simple lesson from the first morning of the course. You'll never persuade anyone to buy anything unless you know exactly what it is that you're selling. That's true not just of hawking widgets and bottles of snake oil – or diamonds and racehorses, come to that – but also of the much trickier business of selling yourself. If you don't know what skills you have to offer, you're hardly going to be able to persuade a potential employer that you have them.

Many of the people who are looking for another place on the treadmill find themselves facing interviewers again for the first time since they were as stupidly young and enthusiastic as I was – and this time, instead of trying to impress some grizzled and cynical old no-hoper who has been sidetracked into what used to be called the personnel department, they are looking across the desk at keen-eyed youngsters who look as though they have just popped out of Chinawhite. Somehow, the generations have got mixed up in the last 30 years. It's not a pleasant experience.

But when I spoke to the professionals about it – I *knew* I had been too hasty in writing off the recruitment consultants and outplacement agencies as shysters and conmen – they were quite reassuring. It's not age, they said – it's the effect of being made redundant. Anyone in that position is likely to need a bit of help with their confidence. Which was fine, although it sounded a bit like my mum, years ago, telling that fresh-faced and credulous stranger that everything would be all right, that he really shouldn't worry, and had he put on a clean shirt? But they had practical advice to offer too, like the thought that people of my age, who hadn't sat for an interview in anger for 30 years or more, should be prepared for some very different questions from the ones we remembered. Instead of giving details about our experience or our work record, we were likely to be asked questions like 'Give us an example of an incident where your negotiating skills were strong,' or given psychometric test papers to complete. The questions, in short, would try to establish what you're good at, rather than what you have done. Like everything else, once you know the rules of the game you're playing, it's easier not to make a fool of yourself.

## PLAYING THE INTERVIEW GAME

I had one old friend who, at 53, was just going through the miserable process of being made redundant – the second time around. The first time it had happened was about fifteen years earlier – and he still remembered the advice he had been given then. 'One of the first things you should do is write yourself a list of the three A's,' he told me one night as we had a pint in a pub. 'Assignment, Action, and Achievement are what interviewers want to hear about – what jobs you've been given to do, how you've carried them out, and exactly what you've learned and achieved in doing them. If you make a list like that, you'll give yourself a very useful tool to use in interviews, and you'll make yourself feel a lot better too.'

Well, I had my doubts about the second part of that advice – there is a limit to how many times you can write down 'Not a lot', 'Not much', and 'Stuff-all', and I can say from personal experience that it doesn't make you feel too good when you've done it. But maybe that's because I heard the advice too late.

'It's important that you should write them down as soon as you can,' my friend said. 'When you've just lost your job is the time when you feel at your lowest, and it's then that you need a reminder of the things you can do successfully– and also, it's frighteningly easy to forget some of them.

Remember, this is the basis of the pitch you are going to be putting to potential new employers, so you want to include all the details you can find – increased sales by 10 per cent, reduced waste by 30 per cent, or won £10 million order. You may not have access to that sort of data after you have actually left – and it looks very good on a CV.'

As if, I thought wryly. I don't have figures like that in my past. But it's good, positive advice, and a sensible way to deal with the prejudices you are likely to find in the interviews. With a little ingenuity, you can use the 3A's Plan to turn the interviewers' strategy to your own use. It's easy to be taken off guard by what they call 'Behavioural competency interviewing' – and easy to assume, too, that anyone who can seriously use jargon like that isn't worth talking to. Well, strangle that latter impulse at birth, and take advantage of the situation.

In this sort of interview, you will be asked what you have done that demonstrated your abilities in team working, managing others, dealing with change, or similar fields. The catch is that unless you are the sort of emotionless human computer that has no friends and spends an unhealthy amount of time on the internet, you have no chance at all of thinking of a good example on the spot – so have a few prepared in advance. The 3A's template will help you pull your ideas together, and a careful look at the original job advertisement should help you to pinpoint exactly what 'competencies' they want you to display. A lot of people, in stammering out an answer, talk about what 'we' did, or what they 'tried to achieve' – but it's best to stick specifically to yourself, and your own role in whatever was done.

What the interviewer will be interested in hearing about is what you actually did achieve, not what you were aiming for. Be positive. And, once you safely have the job, if you want to do me a favour, you could use all your influence to stop people using jargon like 'Behavioural competency' in the future!

It's idle to pretend that anyone over 50 isn't facing an up-hill climb in a job interview. People aren't supposed to be biased against older applicants any more, but anyone who believes that they aren't probably believes in the Easter Bunny and the Tooth Fairy as well. Even the people who are prepared to talk to you will almost certainly have their own agenda neatly filed away at the back of their minds: they won't believe, for instance, that anyone over 45 has any capacity to change or develop or manage a new and different role. For them, your experience – what you *have* done – defines what you *can* do much more tightly than it does when you are younger. One man I know tackled that preconception head-on by going out and doing an Open University degree course in business management to show that he was indeed capable of assimilating new skills. 'What I learned was useful for its own sake, but the qualification didn't make a blind bit of difference,' he told me. The general – and mistaken – view is that a man in his fifties learning something new is a bit like someone who knows how to whip off a tablecloth without breaking the plates on the table – it may be interesting and quite amusing, but he's not someone you want around you all the time. It's also, incidentally, for a certain type of inter-viewer, slightly disturbing – what middle-manager in his thirties wants to appoint someone to a job who is not only older and more experienced than he is, but also possibly brighter and more original as well?

But I'm getting negative – and one very good piece of advice that I was given was to stop being so defensive. 'You can't compare yourself with a 25-year-old – but why would you want to?' asked one recruitment consultant. 'By the time you're in your forties or fifties, you have built up a package of extremely sellable experience, and your employers should know that statistically you're in a sector of the population that won't be coming in with hangovers or taking sick leave.'

Because I say it was good advice doesn't necessarily mean I believe it: I've heard too many stories of people turned down for jobs they were eminently qualified for because they were 'at the wrong stage of their career' (i.e. too old), 'over-qualified' (i.e. too old), or that they didn't 'fit the company profile' (i.e. too old). Call me cynical, but I don't believe laws about age discrimination are going to make young men and women employ old men and women any more enthusiastically than they have done before.

But the message that there should be a bit more edge to the character you present at an interview in your fifties, compared to the anxious rabbit you were 30 years ago, is a good one. In those days, all you had to sell was your enthusiasm and a bag full of shiny new certificates, but now you have experience and ideas – something *different* to offer. With a little bit of research into the company you're talking to, it should be possible to show how your background will fit productively into whatever it is that they do. Whisper it very quietly, and never say that I was the one who said it, but once you know what it is that they want, you can tailor what you have to offer to fit – always remembering that you don't want to end up with a job you didn't really want after all.

You might also be able to demonstrate that you aren't going to be a threat to whoever it is who is interviewing you– after all, if they recruit a good candidate to the company, it ought to reflect well on their judgement, although that is a hard tightrope to walk in an interview. And if they don't give you the job anyway – well, at least you'll feel better about yourself than you would if you had just sat there and felt inadequate.

## THE MYTH OF EXPERIENCE

All that advice, of course, may help people who want to get back into the world of salaries, company car-parks, pension contributions, and P45s – and I certainly don't mean to sound dismissive about that option. The point about it is that if you *do* go return to that world, it should be because you've made a positive choice to do so, not just because you drifted back there. But if you're applying for sticking-plaster jobs to make a few quid while you take stock and work out what you really want to do, then all your executive history and middle-aged gravitas aren't going to be much help. I know from bitter experience that in interviews for those jobs – the sort your children pick up and drop again during the summer months without a second thought, which is a bit galling – it's easy to be too honest. The best tactic is simple: smile a lot, and don't say anything stupid – don't say, for instance, if you want to be a *chocolatier*, that you're likely to eat the stock. That experience still rankles.

And there was another thought that was particularly worth remembering, this time from a man called Gerry who had been made redundant at 58 and now described himself as 'probably the oldest bloke working as a receptionist in the country'. His line was a challenging one. 'Middle-aged people can be their own worst enemies. They carry baggage, they hate change, and they whinge,' he said. 'You can't expect charity because you've been made redundant. You have to look as fresh as possible, and be sure that it doesn't sound as if you're just asking for a retirement job. Show that you have forward-looking attitudes which will be of value to the company – which is easier said than done if you're a member of the cynics' club, as we all are at times.'

It's undoubtedly true, too, that we can sometimes fool ourselves about how valuable our experience is – and that's not only because the world has this unfair habit of changing while we're not looking, so we have to keep learning new tricks just to do the same thing we were managing quite happily only last week. Most doctors, I was told once by a man who trains them and therefore ought to know, believe implicitly that as they get older, more experienced and more sympathetic, they get better at the daunting task of presenting their patients and their patients' families with the bad news they sometimes have to give. The only trouble is, this wise old man explained to me, that by and large, it's not true. They don't get any better at all.

'Giving someone bad news about their prognosis is one of the worst jobs on the ward – and so it's generally given to the most junior doctor. That's human nature,' he said. 'So the young man goes off, feeling miserable, and sits down with the patient and does his best. Quite often, that means simply mumbling a few incoherent platitudes, and then coming out with something like ''I'm sorry, but you're gonna die!''' (I suspect he might have been exaggerating here, but I think I got his point.)

'Of course, the patient is distraught – and so, being the instinctively sympathetic sort of character that generally comes into medicine, is the young doctor. But the next time he does the same thing, he doesn't feel so bad. It's not because he's done the job any better, but simply because he's seen the suffering before. But he goes on from patient to patient, feeling that because *he* feels a little better each time, he must be getting better at breaking the bad news to them.'

So what the young man thinks is experience is in fact simply a gradual deadening of his sympathetic response – and unless someone stops him, he will go into his retirement believing that he has done a good and sensitive job. (My medical student daughter tells me – not for the first time in her life – that I am hopelessly out-of-date, and that these skills *are* taught in medical schools these days – but that still leaves an awful lot of doctors whose experience of medical school is several decades old. The principle still applies.) We're not all doctors, and we don't all face the nightmare of giving people such tragic news – but we all run the risk of believing that simply doing a job for a long time automatically makes us better at it. I have a stack of emails from people of my age complaining indignantly that the adolescent boys and girls who had interviewed them had not shown enough respect for their experience – but reading between the lines, it didn't seem that the people who were complaining had demonstrated a lot of respect for the interviewers either. 'He was hardly out of school, and clearly didn't have the first idea what he was talking about,' complained one man, who hadn't been given the job he had applied for. Well, maybe – but I couldn't help thinking that a little humility on both sides of the desk might have made for a more productive interview.

One more piece of advice that I got from several people was to get myself on a course. 'It doesn't really matter what,' one said. 'Obviously, if you choose something relevant to whatever it is you think you might want to do professionally, then it won't do you any harm to have picked up an extra qualification and a bit more experience – but what it's really about is making yourself feel better.' The Irish poet Patrick Kavanagh once observed that the best way out of the black hole of despondency is to learn something: it may be a new language, or a poem, or the first sixteen decimal places of pi, but the experience of exercising your mind will give a boost to your self-esteem. That's the theory, anyway, and it seems to apply to the post-redundancy blues as much as to any other sort of depression. If it gives you a bit of extra experience with which to impress an interviewer, then so much the better.

It's also worth remembering, incidentally, where the HR departments of the big companies get it wrong. All over the world, people are being told to try and improve the things they aren't good at – but if you're going to learn something, why not take something you *are* good at, and learn to do it better? If you're no good at selling, you're unlikely to turn yourself into a super-salesman, and struggling from being absolutely useless to being slightly worse than average doesn't seem worth the effort. But if you're good at dealing with people, or planning production strategies, or whatever it is that people do in factories – why not make yourself better at it? Companies spend a fortune teaching people to do what they're not good at – but your greatest strength is likely to prove to be your greatest area for growth. And by concentrating on it, you'll certainly make yourself happier, and probably more employable as well.

But if, as we've seen, the people who will be talking to you will be much more interested in what you can do in the future than in what you have done in the past, your experience may not be as important in an interview as you think. Anyway, experience, however impressive it may seem, can be very much a wasting asset. Last week's triumphs may be pretty amazing, but last year's can look a bit dated – and that applies to the biggest names in the world. I remember being in a pub in Bristol where there was great excitement because Ian Botham was having a quiet drink in a downstairs bar. Two teenagers who were with us were less than impressed: 'Who is he, anyway?' one of them asked – he may have been having us on, but his ignorance had the ring of truth. The other one thought for a moment, and then realisation dawned. 'You know,' he said – 'He's that friendly old guy on television – the one who sells Shredded Wheat.'

So in the unlikely event that Ian Botham is looking for a new start, he might be better advised to look for jobs as a salesman rather than anything to do with cricket. It's a cruel old world, whoever you are.

## NOTES

— Assignment, Action, and Achievement — write them down. And don't sell yourself short!

— Concentrate on showing an interviewer how your experience will fit into his company. Nobody else will have exactly your background — show him how much he needs you.

— Learn something — anything. It may look good on a CV — and, even more important, it will make you feel a lot better about yourself.

# Chapter Nine

## Being Your Own Boss

I suppose most people who suddenly find themselves without a job dream at some point of a wonderful future when, having started the new business that will one day make them rich and famous, the middle-ranking number-cruncher who handed them their redundancy notice will grovel before their half-acre desk as they beg and plead for a job in World Widgets Incorporated, the 21st-century equivalent to Microsoft, the Virgin Group and Google all rolled into one – and in a more realistic mood, they may envisage a small but profitable company which will keep them comfortably into their old age.

And, most importantly, they will imagine themselves never having another boss as long as they live. They will work for themselves, and nobody else. There are those for whom stress is the one thing above all that they miss once they walk out of the office door for the last time. For them, once they've been given the heave-ho by a large business, one obvious answer is to start a small one. I suppose my plumbing fantasy might have fitted that bill – but, even forgetting my total inability to connect two pipes together without starting a flood, it would never have been for me. I had certainly had enough of working for other people – but while I had no desire to start pruning roses or developing a mind-destroying fascination for daytime television, the idea of lying awake at night worrying about the profit and loss account of Andrew Taylor Enterprises Ltd filled me with horror. No-one in my entire life has ever trusted me with money – not, I hope, because they don't think I'm honest, but because I have always been pathologically incapable of counting the small change in my pocket twice and making it come to the same amount.

That was going to have to change. I wasn't planning to set up a small business in the sense of painting my name on the side of a van, or screwing a brass plate to the wall outside, but however I was going to earn my own money, I was going to have to master some of the skills of the businessman. The old days of leaving it all up to the grumpy little gnomes and leprechauns who slave away in the accounts department and grumble about your expenses were well and truly gone.

After all, other people had managed it, from the chap who comes round to clean my windows to the man who founded Waterstone's – he had got that off the ground with £6,000 of the redundancy money that WH Smith had paid him, and gone on to create a bookshop that had put theirs in the shade. So there was a wide range of possibilities to aim for – although, to be realistic, Tim Waterstone had raised another £100,000 of venture capital to back his idea. Since I have trouble borrowing money to pop down to the pub, the chances of talking people into that kind of largesse seemed slim – so perhaps I would be looking at the bucket-and-sponge end of the spectrum.

## SETTING OUT ON YOUR OWN

The scary statistic is that around 60 per cent of new businesses fold within three years – and that doesn't count the ones that struggle on without ever making any money, turning gradually from a vibrant young business into a semi-obsessive hobby, and finally into a millstone locked firmly around the neck of the would-be entrepreneur. There are obvious difficulties: for people in their twenties and thirties, for example, there is the problem of finance and the risk of dragging down their new business with over-borrowing. That's a problem that may grow less acute with age; by the time they are in their forties or fifties, many people will have built some capital in their house, or they'll have their savings, or even their redundancy payment to give their business plans a kick start – and they will also have two or three decades of experience banked away as well.

To anyone who is coming new to the idea of running a small business it can sound pretty daunting – after all, when you talk about betting the farm on something, or putting your pension on it, it's generally a figure of speech. Starting your own business is the one area where it can be all too literally true. But in theory, having that cash behind them ought to give older people a big advantage. It ought to be plain sailing – except that all too many of them don't do their homework. All the experts I spoke to agreed that the one over-riding reason why new businesses fail is that the would-be entrepreneurs don't think their plans through carefully enough or do enough research into the best ways to make them work.

What's the competition? How much can you charge? Does the business plan work? The one thing that all the experts agree on about starting out on your own is that after you think you have finished doing your research, you should do some more. And then some more again.

And when you've finished doing your research into your market, how you can fill a gap in it, and how the financial sums work out – in fact, you've never finished digging out answers to those questions, so let's say when you can take a bit of time off from it – you can do a bit more research into yourself. When you look back on your working life, for instance, do you ever feel that you have been something of an impostor? That you weren't quite as competent as everybody thought? (In fact, this is a trick question: if you answered 'No', then I don't believe you. Almost everyone, in the deepest quiet of the night, wonders to themselves sometimes whether they will eventually be found out. Some people cope with it better then others, that's all.) Well, if confidence is a big issue for you, then perhaps working for yourself, or running your own business, is not a sensible move – because you will get challenges to your self-image pretty much all the time.

But that's only the first of a series of questions you need to ask yourself – not so much about what you want, this time, as about what you need. Are you a person who needs company, or do you relish the idea of days spent on your own in front of a computer screen? Are you going to fret about not having a regular monthly income? If climbing a company ladder has been important to you – ticking off the boxes as you move into the bigger office, walk on the deeper-pile carpet and pee in a more luxurious loo – then, once again, running your own business may not be for you. You're not only going to be climbing the ladder, you're going to be building it as well, propping it up against the wall, and making sure it doesn't fall down.

## THE FREELANCE GAME – HAVE PC, WILL TRAVEL

So how important is independence going to be to you? I have spent too much of my life working for people whose bones I wouldn't grind to make cat litter, and the idea of never having another boss again made my eyes shine with anticipation. The *Aftershock* column, I reasoned, had given me a start in the world of freelancing: never again, I told myself, would I have to work for anybody I didn't like. No reasons, no excuses – if the phone rang, and I didn't like the sound of the voice on the other end, I would just be able to say 'No thank you' and put the phone down. It doesn't, of course, work quite like that: when you are working for yourself, you have not one boss but dozens, and unless you are supremely confident, you need to keep them all happy. At least in the early days, all those fiercely independent thoughts tend to wilt under the stress of wondering whether you are going to be able to fill your week – I had always promised myself that I would never involve myself with a tobacco company, until one actually rang me up soon after I started working for myself and asked me to do some work for them. The moral argument in my mind took less than a moment – but it was long enough for my tongue to have said 'Yes, of course' just before my conscience could frame the question, 'How dare you make me such an insulting offer?'

Other people may do better at sticking to their principles, and it may well be true that I am a man of singularly weak moral fibre – but the reality is that, although you may tell yourself that you can say no to anyone, it's only people like David Beckham who are in so much demand that they can really choose who they work for – and look how that turned out. One way or another, running a business or working for yourself is going to be about making compromises: if it's stress that you want, then you'll get it in spades.

On the other hand, being on your own means that you get to make the decisions about your life, rather than anyone else. You don't need to set up a major business operation to start out as a freelance. One bleak email I received from an *Aftershock* reader had stuck in my mind. After several months and more than three hundred letters of application, she had given up writing off to potential employers. 'Anyone over 50 who looks at the job advertisements is kidding themselves,' she said. Whatever the law says about age discrimination, many companies are reluctant to employ new recruits if they are in their fifties – but while they may not want to give them a job on the staff and a place in the pension scheme, they are quite happy to use their skills on a freelance basis. In those circumstances, all that matters is how well they do the job.

## FRANCHISING – BUSINESS WITHOUT TEARS?

There is another sort of half-way house for the nervous entrepreneur who fancies running his own business, but doesn't enjoy the pressure – a way of riding piggy-back on someone else's ideas and risk-taking. There's a price to be paid for it, of course, but if you set up a business in an established franchise operation, you do at least have a road map to follow and a help-line to call when things seem to be turning remorselessly belly-up. I was introduced to the idea at a funeral – which, cold-blooded as it may seem, is a pretty good place for networking. Perhaps it's something to do with contemplating eternity and the futility of life, or perhaps it's simply that people are searching desperately for something to say – but funerals seem to encourage confidences and the passing on of ideas.

To be honest, it was a bit spooky. There I was, standing outside the church with that inappropriately solemn face with which you remember a man who was always wreathed in smiles, when a friend I hadn't seen for some time came up and tapped me on the arm. 'Have you ever thought of potatoes?' he asked me, quietly.

It wasn't a question that I had been expecting, so I might have paused for a moment, inadvertently giving him the chance for a follow-up. 'Jacket potatoes, I mean. Or lawns? Lawns are very big at the moment. But there is virtually no limit to what you can do.' By now, I was glancing around for the men in white coats, convinced that my friend had been driven mad by grief. And then he explained.

'Franchises, I mean. I know you're looking for a job, and franchises are just about the best way for a person without a lot of business experience to start up a new operation.' Well, 'without a lot of business experience' describes me pretty well – in fact, it exaggerates the extent of my financial and commercial background, which extends no further than once running the college bar and being the first person ever to make a substantial loss in that simplest of businesses – so I was interested.

The idea he was putting forward was simple enough – you hand over an initial franchise fee, and then you use the name, the business model and the know-how of the parent company to operate within your own area. You may be selling jacket potatoes at fairs and other outdoor events, or looking after people's lawns, cleaning their carpets or restoring their furniture – but whatever it is, you will be operating your own company, and making your own profits.

There are comfortably over 30,000 franchise units operating in the UK, employing a total of over 360,000 people, and turning over more than £10 billion a year, so there are clearly plenty of people who believe in it as a way of doing business – especially since, on average, they need £44,000 just to get started.

What they are buying, apart from the name and reputation of the company selling them the franchise, is the experience of making the business work. Someone has run it before, and made the mistakes, and they pass that knowledge on to you – for a fee. It's an idea that people get very passionate about – a tempting short-cut into the world of the independent entrepreneur. But there are drawbacks: depending on the franchise deal you get, you're likely to be paying out a large slice of your potential profits to the company that sold you the franchise in the first place, and as your company grows, you'll be limited in the ways in which you can develop it. If you were hoping to get away from the world in which you have a boss telling you what to do, you could just find yourself in a new one where you have a whole company on your back.

On the plus side, the banks obviously think franchising can be a good way to take that daunting first step – even to people like me, they will typically lend up to 70 per cent of the initial investment, which is a much bigger proportion than they would consider for most start-ups. Or so they say – but first, of course, I needed a pretty fair idea of what sort of franchise appealed to me.

One man I know had been running a furniture repair business for the last eight years, after being made redundant from a career in IT and construction. So that seemed hopeful – it looked on the surface as though it was possible to take the training that they offered and start off with no experience at all. Wrong. One thing I had never known about this friend was that his father was a cabinet-maker, and he spent much of his childhood helping out in the workshop, which must have given him a bit of a start. And when he told me that, he spelt out in bleak and brutal detail just what kind of things I would need to be able to do: experience in working with wood and carpenters' tools, it seems, is just the beginning.

'You have to be realistic about what your skills are, because at least to start with, you need to be a jack of all trades in terms of running the business. You have to be your own IT expert, your own accountant, and most of all, your own marketing manager,' he said. 'And research is important: don't just take what the franchising company tells you at face value. It's a good idea to go out on the road with someone who is actually running the franchise you are interested in, so you can see for yourself how it works before you commit yourself.'

Franchising gives you a start – but it can't avoid all the challenges of setting up your own business. Even the biggest names won't bring customers to your door on their own – you have to go out looking for them and selling yourself. People who set up their own independent business, whether it is stitching parachutes or making chocolate-covered nuts, are generally passionate about stitching, parachutes, nuts or chocolate – they choose to go into areas that interest them. People starting franchises, on the other hand, are buying into someone else's dream.

I spoke to a couple of experts in the field, and they gave me a bucketful of chilly reality. 'You would have to do a lot of research, just like any other business start-up,' they told me. 'What would your customer base be, for instance? What is the competition? How will customers buy whatever it is you are going to be selling?'

'Just because a franchise works well in one part of the country doesn't mean it will succeed somewhere else. The franchise model is brilliant if you do it well, but you need an entrepreneurial vision to see it through successfully.'

So my friend at the funeral was mistaken – franchises aren't a get-rich-quick ticket for anyone with a redundancy cheque in his pocket and the business sense of a lemon. They may not require a Harvard MBA to run them, but like any other business, they need start-up capital, painstaking research, and lots of hard work and dedication. I wasn't scared of the hard work, and I reckoned I could manage the research – but running my own IT, or dealing with the accounts? I could no more swim the Channel.

## WORKING FOR YOURSELF – THE PLUS SIDE

Even for those who are braver, or more talented, or more determined than I am, there are obviously drawbacks to running your own business, whether you take the franchise route or strike out on your own like some would-be Richard Branson. While your pay cheque comes in regularly and predictably each month when you are on the payroll, anyone who works for himself has to do the job, then write an invoice, and then hope that it gets paid – sometime. It can feel as if you're having to work three times for the same money. But on the other hand, there are unexpected benefits which can suddenly become clearer. Where a long-term salaried job with the same company can easily turn into routine, working for yourself can bring a whole series of new challenges. The old friend who told me that said he had never thought about it before, but those challenges were what had always excited him about work. He'd been made redundant a couple of years earlier, and was working for two or three different clients as a freelance interim manager – and it suited him.

'A couple of projects I've been running have gone really well, and one of the clients asked me whether I wouldn't rather be working for them full time – a big outfit with money to spend and lots of status. It was very flattering, but then

I thought "Why would I want to do that?'" he said. 'The excitement is in turning something new around, sorting the problems out, and seeing it start to work properly – those are the things that give me a buzz about coming to work.' That buzz, incidentally, cost him tens of thousands of pounds a year, because he earned considerably less than he would have done for the big company he scorned – but he never had a second thought about that. 'I earn enough – and I look forward to each new job. I don't know many big-shot executives who can say the same,' he said.

And there was another benefit, which became clearer as he moved through his fifties. 'I'm never going to retire in the way my dad did,' he told me. 'There isn't going to be a day when I will stop work and go home with a gold watch: I'll gradually work a few days less here and there, and probably a few hours less in each day, until eventually I'm just working every now and then, when I feel like it.'

'I used to worry about what I would do when I stopped work – and then when it happened and they made me redundant, it was too soon for me to retire, so I was forced into working for myself like this. I never realised that this would be one of the side-effects, but now I'm in charge of what I do much more than I would have been if I'd still been drawing a salary.' He could decide for himself how much money he wanted to earn, and how much time he wanted to have off.

He had one other thought too: the crucial thing, what-ever you're doing with your new life, is to reach the stage where you stop comparing it with what went before. 'Yes, I'm earning less than I was, and yes, I have a lot more satisfaction than I had before. But I just don't think about those things any more. That's the way life used to be – always measuring yourself against some yardstick or other, to see how well you were doing in your career. But now I don't think about those days at all. This is the life I have now, and I'm looking forward, not back.'

I was impressed, and I knew just how he felt – but I could feel an icy dribble of realism running down my spine, as if someone had just slipped an ice-cube down the back of my neck. These, after all, were people who had some ex-perience of running a business, which I hadn't; they weren't surprised by succeeding. I was different; I couldn't sell nuts to monkeys, and I knew it. The world seems to divide fairly convincingly into those who expect to succeed in business and those who expect to fail. I decided then and there that I definitely fit into the latter group – and I've never been disappointed yet.

## NOTES

— Ask yourself if you can honestly cope with the stress of running your own business.
— Is franchising the answer?
— Remember the three R's — Research, Research, and Research.

# Chapter Ten

## A Brief Stopover in Hell

One of the things I'd been doing right from the start was trawling around the internet – to be honest, 'trawling the internet' was, during the bad times, often a euphemism for playing completely unproductive computer games, but amongst the Sudoku and online Scrabble, I had found several websites aimed specifically at people in just my position. One of them, flatteringly, announced that it had originally been inspired by the *Aftershock* column – but all of them agreed on one thing. When it came to looking for help, finding a new job, or searching for that elusive Great Idea which would change your life, the most important thing was to cast your net as wide as possible. I needed, I realised, to take their advice. I needed – horrible word – to start networking.

## NETWORKING – SOCIAL TORTURE OF THE 21ST CENTURY

There is no way out of it: if you are thinking of working for yourself, you need to go out and look for clients or customers, and if you're looking for another job being paid by someone else, you have to put yourself about to find the opportunities. But for anyone who has a soul that is not crafted from chips of ice, there are problems with networking. There is, for example, that chilly moment when you walk into a room crowded with strangers, and see in each face the same wide-eyed rabbit-like desperation that you know is mirrored in your own – the desperation caused by the terror of looking desperate. Everyone wants to give the impression of being casual and on top of their game – and nobody does.

Many of the placement companies organise networking parties, while others are set up by self-help groups – but they all have the same aim. They exist to get you talking to people who might be able to help you, and whom you might never have run into otherwise. One of the parties I dragged myself to presented me with an additional problem: the hosts had very thoughtfully given the guests name badges to wear slung around their necks, to make introductions easier. And a very good thing too – except that for anyone of my age and height, it involved leaning forward and peering short-sightedly into a succession of indignant cleavages. I might have got away with it 30 years ago, but I suspect I was lucky to leave the premises without a police escort, a thick lip, and a lifetime entry in the sex offenders register.

These parties are a bit like speed-dating – a quick five minutes to see if you can do each other a favour, and then move on rapidly to the next target. The subject of joblessness hangs over the evening like an unfortunate smell – no-one likes to mention it, but it's never far from anyone's thoughts. Some people bounce and bubble frenetically, as if they are trying to prove how confident and irrepressible they are, while others have a sort of death's head seriousness about them: however important and respected they may have been in their past lives, redundancy has a way of stripping them naked in company. David wrote to me from Nottingham describing an experiment he had tried shortly before his notice ran out and he had to leave his high-powered management job.

His networking efforts had started badly, because the contacts book he had once prided himself on had become very thin. 'Corporate life can make you relatively lazy in terms of cultivating contacts,' he said. 'If I only had known a few years ago what I know now!'

The experiment was to see how he could cope with the networking nightmare if he was stripped of what he called his 'no-fear uniform' – his business cards and his status as a managing director – and the results were scary. 'I have never had any fear of dealing with senior directors in my present job, because my position and my business card make me credible. There have never been any issues of self-confidence or gravitas to worry about,' he said. 'But last week, I went to a conference, and deliberately treated it as a rehearsal for the real world. I left behind the corporate protection of the business cards that had my role as managing director printed on them – and what a difference I found!' People he would normally have stood and chatted with quite happily turned into demons that he couldn't approach; his confidence simply drained away.

And he wasn't alone. Networking parties are probably the worst social torture invented since the Roman emperors were dishing out invitations to their 'Christians and Lions' celebrations. If the clerics of the Spanish Inquisition had thrown cocktail parties, they might have been very like a modern networking session – although with better wine, obviously.

They don't even offer the usual party refuge of another drink, partly because you know it's going to taste like anti-freeze, and partly because, for some reason, high-powered executives don't seem to consider it a satisfactory business introduction when you are sick over their shoes. Even getting slightly tipsy is a complete no-no. So, having made your obligatory and stone-cold sober three circuits of the room, fiddled with your glass of wine and stuffed yourself with as many canapés as you can decently manage, you leave with a pocketful of business cards to make your way home – hopefully not in the back of a police transit.

Talking to the experts, the idea is that you then sit at your computer as soon as you arrive home, and sort your new contacts into different categories – immediate job prospects, possible future ones, people who might be able to offer help and advice. And then, over the next few days, you start phoning round them, cementing the new friendships, maybe even sending them a CV, until someone who was impressed by your charm, intelligence and funny stories at the party offers you the job you have been dreaming about for months. Well, I said that was the idea.

## THEORY AND REALITY

Outplacement agencies and networking groupies actually draw up little charts for you to follow, with arrows, asterisks and bizarre underlinings to mark out the different categories of contacts you should be following up. Your primary contacts – your A-list, if you want to use the language of Victoria Beckham, Tom Cruise, Paris Hilton and the networking pros – is made up of the people who know you and rate your abilities, even if they don't have great networking potential. They will do their best to pass you on to their own primary contacts, who will become your B-list. Then *they* will pass you on to *their* contacts who become your C-list, and so on, right down the alphabet, until you come to the sort of Z-listers who turn up on Celebrity Love Island and have pictures of their charming homes in gruesome magazines. One risk, I imagine, is that the chain might work rather like the game of Chinese whispers, so that by the time you reach the end of the chain you are an entirely different person from the one who started out at the top of it – but you'll have noticed by now that I don't take all this malarkey entirely seriously.

The reality, in my experience at least, is slightly different. You get home from the party feeling bloated and grumpy, collapse into bed and then, two or three days later, remember that you have a bundle of dog-eared cards still cluttering up your pocket. You shuffle through them more or less at random, and find that you can't remember which card goes with which half-remembered face. You gaze blankly at the occasional note scrawled in biro on the back of a card, unable to read it and unable to understand it if you could, and you desperately try to remember who said what, and how promising it sounded. You make two or three tentative phone calls, and find that two of the people who answer can't remember you, and the third is a dog's home somewhere in Barnsley, because you've scribbled the number down wrongly. In fact, although this may say more about my own shortcomings than about the system, I don't think I have ever made a single useful contact at a networking party.

## LEARNING HOW TO HANDLE HELL

Just as I was grumbling about my latest excursion into network-party hell, I ran into a piece of straight talking from a friend who had more good sense than kindness. 'So learn how to handle them,' he said. I think he had simply had enough of my whingeing.

'Just what sort of a dork do you think I am?' This was a dangerous sort of question, inviting a much more detailed analysis of my personal failings than I might usually welcome, but it was the only possible response to the suggestion that had just been put to me. I like to see myself as an ordinary sort of chap, who goes to the pub occasionally, who has friends, and knows a few jokes. I do not spend long, lonely hours playing computer games or having intimate virtual conversations on vaguely disreputable internet sites; I do not wear misshapen cardigans with holes in the sleeves; and I do not have embarrassing personal hygiene problems.

I do not, thank you very much indeed, need to go on a course to get advice on how to make friends. 'So stop whingeing,' he said, with chilly politeness, and the sort of smile you could drop into a gin and tonic.

Which is how I came to be sitting sulkily at the start of a one-day course, along with seven other would-be social butterflies of the networking circuit, arms folded across my chest in a bit of classic and unmistakeable 'leave me alone' body language. If I'm honest, I was rather ashamed of the fact that I couldn't handle the networking circus – after all, in comparison to people who face down muggers in the street, or dash into burning buildings, chatting for five minutes to some overweight oil executive is hardly an example of medal-winning courage under fire. But I really didn't think that I needed a course in how to make friends.

Reassuringly, it didn't turn out to be like that – it was more about dealing with new contacts than making new friends. The other people in the group didn't seem to be Johnny No-Mateses either – quite the reverse, in fact. There were eight of us, four men and four women – a couple of salesmen, four middle-ranking management types, and one member of the administrative staff at a university. And me. I realised with a sinking feeling that I was not only the oldest one there – although there was a whole range of ages, from late twenties up – I was also the only one who was actually looking for a job.

But the brisk and businesslike former actress who was running the course clearly didn't have much time for self-pity. 'Don't worry about that. Something like one in eight of our clients – one from each course – is either looking for a job or about to change,' she said. And in fact, when we were all chatting, I fibbed anyway – so no-one else on the course knew I didn't have a job too.

It was all good, practical stuff – lots of role plays, practising things like ways of joining or leaving groups, pitching your voice so that it doesn't grate with the people you're talking to, and noting the different effect that a change in your tone of voice can have on the person listening to you. If you had asked me, I would have said that I would rather rip my right arm off than go through play-acting like that in public – but when everyone was doing it, it was good fun. I enjoyed the day. But does it work? Does it make a difference to how you perform in those buttock-clenchingly embarrassing moments when you have nothing to say to a person who doesn't interest you at a party you're not enjoying?

The organisers say it does, but then they would, wouldn't they? So do the people I spoke to who had done the course before me – they reckoned it had given them more confidence, and enabled them to enjoy events that they would otherwise have dreaded. From my own experience, I can see what they mean, although using the word 'enjoyment' about a networking event seems a bit over-optimistic. And I did come away with one useful piece of practical advice about handing over business cards – the trick is always to write something on a card before you hand it over to someone. It doesn't matter whether you add an extra phone number to the one on the card, or jot down the date or the place where you handed it over – if there is something written there, people are much more likely to look at it, rather than leaving it on their desk for three months before throwing it in the bin. And yes, it does work, because I've tried it.

But is handing out business cards more effectively, or chatting to people without feeling that my tongue is stuck in treacle, or that my arms and legs are too big for my body, going to help me find a job? The courses that offer to teach you 'influencing skills' and 'communication dynamics' in a day – and there are plenty of them to find on the internet – cost around £400. That may not be a fortune in the context of a job-search that could last for months, but it's enough out of the monthly budget to make you stop and think.

Maybe it's all to do with self-image: being told that you need help and guidance in getting on with people seems only a very little better than being on the receiving end of one of those appalling deodorant advertisements from the 1970s where cheesy actors murmur the letters 'B ... O' coyly in your ear. I can tell jokes, dammit; I can smile and chat to people. Why would I want a course that claims to make me a nicer person at a party? It's a weakness in me, of course, and probably one of many reasons why I will never be rich; after all, if making contacts is as crucially important as it obviously is, why would anyone not want to get better at it? What's not to like?

## USING THE CONTACTS YOU'VE GOT

But the good news is that the parties-from-hell aren't an unavoidable first step on the networking trail. The network I used most intensively, right from the start, was my own personal one. What were those first nervous calls to my friends for reassurance if they weren't the start of a networking campaign? It may be less glamorous than some big city party with drinks and canapés, but it's also much less scary: the way to begin is on your own, with a tele-phone. After all, in 30 years of conscientiously marching into a succession of offices, I reckoned, most people would have picked up a number of friends they can trust. If they haven't, then they have bigger problems than redundancy to worry about, and they probably really do need to get out more. But you have to be prepared to play a long game. The advice from several employment consultants I spoke to was to draw up a list of 20 people you could go and talk to – and then do whatever it takes to get to go and see them. You're not necessarily going to ask them for a job – although I couldn't help thinking that it might be nice if they just offered me one – but instead, you want their advice about what your priorities ought to be, and another set of views about what you have to offer a potential employer.

I've never been able to think of the mates I have picked up over the years as 'contacts,' but I used them shame-lessly over the first few months after I was made redundant.

Some studies suggest that fewer than 10 per cent of new jobs are ever formally advertised – all the rest are filled by word of mouth. The figures may be suspect – how can you calculate something like that? – but the principle is probably true, especially for people who aren't straight out of university and filling in application forms for graduate traineeships. If you're looking for a job, then the employ-ment pages of the newspapers will only take you so far. You have to go out there looking – and there are all sorts of benefits to be gained from the search. You might just hit gold and find someone you used to know who has made his million and wants a personal assistant at £200,000 a year – but it's not a good idea to count on it, unless you once happened to live next door to Bill Gates or the Sultan of Brunei. (I can save your time by telling you that they don't need highly paid, unqualified personal assistants. I know. I asked already.) But what is more likely is that they may have a suggestion of a possible avenue for you to follow, or an idea of some freelance work that might suit you. Perhaps, with your name freshly in their mind, they might drop it into a conversation of their own sometime after you speak to them – but probably the most useful help they are likely to give you is their fresh insight into what your capabilities and talents really are. If they open up new possibilities in your mind, then they will have done you a huge favour. If that works, you may find it changes your ideas and helps you work out exactly what it is that you want – that crucial question again.

You don't always have to be asking for help when you pick up the phone, either – it can be a sophisticated sort of bartering, which profits you and the person you're calling. 'I'm good at that, you're good at this – why don't we get together?' How many careers have been built on that sort of deal?

And there are other, even more personally rewarding, ways of using networking too. Another guest at the party I was at had been made redundant as Chief Executive of a medium-sized company a few years before. In his old life, he said, he'd had head-hunters ringing him up periodically, calling four or five times in a morning in the hope of getting five minutes of his time. He'd had eager young executives wanting to send him their CVs, in the hope that he might find them a role. Now, none of them even returned his calls. We've all been there, of course – but he wasn't downhearted. 'Listen,' he said, bending forward slightly, and smiling a smile that would have chilled the soul of Caligula, 'I don't have a job now, but I will have one day. And I'll remember the people who speak to me now, and the ones who don't. I have a list of them, and I won't forget.'

What goes around, in short, really does come around. It's a very cheering thought, as you pick up the telephone to make the fortieth call.

## NOTES

— Your book of contacts is the most precious thing you have — a friend in need is the quickest way to find a new job.

— Do as I say, not as I do: follow up the new contacts you make as quickly as you can.

— You may be able to avoid the torture of networking parties — but you have to put yourself about. Most jobs are never advertised.

# Chapter Eleven

## The Money Man

I am not stupid. I know I have been talking about things like fulfilment and happiness as if I had just stepped out of a sixties commune. I do believe in these things, and I think I kept pretty much focused on them while I was blundering around looking for a new future. But there is another consideration as well, which may be less entertaining to think about, but still kept pushing its ugly little snout into my mind.

*Money.*

## ANOTHER BIG QUESTION

You'll remember that the first big question was 'What do you want?' – and if the answer to it was simply 'Money', then you're not likely to have read this far. Now we're looking at a different question: What do you need?

For most people, whether they admit it or not, money comes pretty high up the list of priorities throughout their lives. You don't need to be a red-in-tooth-and-claw bloated capitalist to want to keep a roof over your family's head and a meal on the table – but one of the advantages of growing up is that you can take a longer view: you can work out how *much* you need, and exactly what you are prepared to sacrifice to get it. There are people in their twenties and thirties who would climb over their grannies' heads in order to climb a little higher up the ladder. (I know there are – just ask my granny.) No doubt such people, who would think they had got a good deal if they dropped their own eyes into a blender in order to get a pay rise, still exist in the world of the 40- and 50-year-olds, but they seem to be fewer and further between.

I had short-term commitments, such as two children in university and another on the way there. There was the big medium-term one of a mortgage hanging around my neck, but like many people my age, I could begin to see the dim outline in the distance of a time when that would be paid off and forgotten about. And over everything loomed the long-term shadow of the pension. Here, perhaps, I had something of an unfair advantage – not in terms of the generosity of my existing pension contributions, which were minuscule, the sort of figures that make a financial adviser either laugh or cry, depending on how much he likes you – but in my personal history. Cancer isn't an experience that is awash with advantages, but when you have spent some time lying on your back and contemplating the possibility that you might not reach 50, the prospect of reaching 70 without much money becomes a bit less daunting. Old age, under any conditions at all, becomes an ambition rather than something to be feared – a dream, not a nightmare.

So I wasn't as worried as many people are about the threat of poverty in my old age; my children would soon be happily paying for themselves; my mortgage, if I could only keep feeding the beast for a few more years, would eventually vanish in a puff of smoke; and my pension – well, that would look after itself. After all, if you are as superstitious as I sometimes am, a large pension pot stashed away for your old age can begin to seem a bit like a deliberate provocation to Fate. The best way to make God laugh is to say to yourself that you have the future safely sorted. Everybody told me that this was an extremely irresponsible attitude, and I'm sure they were right. Even so, although no doubt there would be some unpleasant surprises in the next few years, as far as I could see, I didn't actually *need* as much money as I had thought at first. I didn't want to make myself a lifelong slave to consumption, and I didn't have to.

## A REALITY CHEQUE

Well, that's what *I* thought. I didn't want to see a financial adviser, and I didn't think there was any need to, even though I've always had only the haziest idea of what I've got, even less about what I need, and no idea at all about how to work out what the difference between the two might be. I've always thought of the bank as figuratively, as well as literally, a four-letter word. The first time I ever saw a financial adviser, he persuaded me to sell several years in a very well-funded final salary pension scheme in return for a few pieces of paper which will entitle me, sometime in my nineties, to just about enough money to buy a round of drinks and a bag of crisps once a year. I have friends who occasionally murmur 'It's an Equitable Life, Henry' with a bitter laugh as they contemplate the huge black hole where their pension was growing.

So I am not a good customer for investment brokers or money-magicians. The second time I'd looked for advice about money, back in those far-off days when I'd had a regular income, the first subject that had been put on the table was whether I was aware that there would shortly be a government ceiling on how much I could have in my pension scheme. I wasn't, of course, but when my new friend told me that the ceiling was going to be set at £1.5 million, I realised that we were communicating across a universe of incomprehension from one planet to another. What I needed was gritty advice about what I could afford to do, not pipe dreams about dodging the tax on limitless wealth in my old age. All in all, I wasn't particularly enthusiastic about financial advisers.

But everybody else seemed to be. My friends, my family, my other half, all told me that a financial adviser should have been one of my first ports of call after I started out on my own. I'd probably left it too late, they said, but it was better late than never – and they dragged me by the hair, kicking, screaming and clutching at files of hopelessly out-of-date bank statements and credit card bills, to see what a little financial advice could do for me.

The first thing I discovered, to my relief, was that I wasn't alone. Financial advisers, it seems, are like dentists – we all know we ought to go, but we keep on putting it off. With the instinct for stupidity that makes the smug phrase *Homo sapiens* the original contradiction in terms, we tend to do that with even more determination at times when we most need to get our finances in order – times like the ones I was going through. Nobody, after all, likes to hear bad news, and the news about your finances when you have just lost your job is unlikely to be particularly cheery.

But the advice I got was exactly the sort of practical thinking I needed – not a word about £1.5 million pension ceilings, but instead, a crisp five-point checklist of what I ought to be doing. Sorting out my pension, not surprisingly, was near the top of the list of priorities – but it wasn't *at* the top. 'The first thing you should do is work out a budget – work out what you actually need in financial terms,' I was told. 'You can go through your bank statements for the past few months, and take out any expenses that you won't have in the future – things like season tickets or costs related to your job. It's not a precise science, and there is an awful lot of guesswork involved, but that's a start.'

This conversation wasn't particularly cheap – the whole deal worked out at around £750 – and there was something vaguely embarrassing about being gently lectured about my financial shortcomings by a man young enough to be my son. But it was valuable stuff. Once I had sorted out some sort of rudimentary budget, I had to check up on what state my pension fund was in. (I could answer that one quite quickly: Dire.) Then it was the pension that had been built up by my spouse, as the adviser charmingly insisted on calling her, and after that, a list of any big expenses I could foresee – children's weddings, for instance, or university fees. And finally, the big one that no-one wants to confront: Debt.

'That's the one people often forget, and it can really cause problems,' I was told. 'If you want to retire, or work part-time, you may have to downsize to clear your mort-gage, or you may have a redundancy payment to clear it ('As if!' I thought, with a wry smile) but it's crucial that you are in control of your debts.' Now, I am a man who should be kept away from credit cards like small boys are kept away from AK-47 machine guns. I am in control of my debt in the same way that those hare-brained cowboys that you see showing off at rodeos in the movies are in control of their bucking broncos: I long ago gave up any hope of one day leading it sedately round the paddock, and have pretty well settled for clinging on grimly for dear life and hoping that eventually it doesn't shake me off into the dust with a bone-shattering crunch. I am the only person I know who trembles with fear when he gets a cheque in the post, because I know with an awesome certainty that if I receive £10 after breakfast, I will assuredly have spent £15 by lunch. I don't need a financial adviser to tell me to take control of my debt as much as I need a surgeon to separate me from my credit card and a squad of SAS soldiers to stop me from going to the cash machine.

I am, in short, the man that Dickens's Mr Micawber was thinking of when he warned: 'Annual income twenty pounds, annual expenditure twenty pounds ought and six, result misery' – except that so far, more by luck than judgment, I have somehow managed to avoid most of the misery. What I have done instead is give the bank a grotesque proportion of the money I have earned in my life in return for lending me some more – enough, as I pointed out to my children as they set off for university and eventual financial independence, to have bought myself a nice new Saab convertible for my 45<sup>th</sup> birthday, if only I had been putting the money into a jam jar instead of into the profits of the National Westminster Bank. What they will eventually carve on my gravestone is – well, not much, because there will be nothing in my bank account to pay the stonemason.

There are plenty of people around who will offer advice on what to do with a redundancy cheque, if you are lucky enough to have one, from employment consultants who want to take a slice of it in return for putting you on their computer files to get-rich-quick merchants offering you dodgy internet deals. When you come into money in any way at all, whether through inheriting it from wealthy parents, taking it off Chris Tarrant on *Who Wants to be a Millionaire*, or picking up the fabled redundancy cheque that is going to end all your worries, the people at the bank who were so hard to get hold of the day before suddenly keep ringing you up as if they were asking you out on a date.

But for my money, the five-point plan I had been offered sounded like a good place to start – and other people I spoke to thought so too. Colin, from Bradford, had been made redundant around the same time as me, and although he still had no idea what he was going to do, he had already started planning what to do with the pay-off he'd got – not a big cheque as these things go, but comfortably above the £15,000 or so legal minimum he was entitled to. 'I know I'm going to have to move into somewhere smaller. I'd planned to do that anyway in a few years' time, but now I'll have to do it sooner rather than later,' he said. 'But I'm lucky – at least I'll be able to pay off the mortgage, and start again with a clean slate.' Anything left over, he said, would go into his pension fund.

If my financial health check had been a real medical one, then I would have ended up in intensive care, with a rats' nest of plastic tubes dangling out of me, and a box of electronic wizardry beeping quietly in the corner, while people tiptoed past and spoke in hushed tones. There were no nice surprises – but on the other hand, there were no heart-rending shocks either. I walked away from it with a fairly clear idea of where I stood, which is much better than worrying about it. Financial consultancy is a bit like being a professional wet blanket: people turn up with their dreams and ambitions, and the consultant picks them apart, holds them up in the air between his finger and thumb, wrinkles his nose, and says that you can't afford them. But perhaps that's a bit cynical – it's really a question of making the dreams and the reality fit. I'm clearly not going to be worrying about the £1.5 million pension ceiling for a year or two, but with a bit of care, I might just be sitting up in bed in the financial intensive care unit before too long and asking for a drink.

## NOTES

— You may think you don't need an independent financial adviser. You're wrong.

— Sit down with him and work out your budget — what you have and what you need. No, I said need, not want — you may be pleasantly surprised.

— Work through the five-point check list: Budget, Pension, Partner's Pension, Big Expenses, Debt.

# Chapter Twelve

## Rattling a Tin

**G**ood ideas don't always follow each other in the way that you'd expect. It was quite ironic that, just after my meeting with the money man, I should have had one of my best and most productive thoughts – that had absolutely nothing to do with making any money. It was also nearly twelve months after The Fax – not particularly quick, perhaps, but I guess it was a marathon, not a sprint, that I was starting out on. I'm not sure what sparked my brainwave, but it came at a fairly low point, when I was beginning to think that I could write the thinking person's guide to coping with rejection letters – the sort in which the first paragraph is full of how wonderful you are, and the second starts with the word 'However', or 'Unfortunately'. Over the past few weeks, I'd usually found one technique was to repeat under your breath the words 'I didn't want to work for the jerks anyway' as I screwed the letter up very small indeed and lobbed it into the bin. That usually worked quite well, especially if I injected the right amount of venom into the words.

For dealing with people who asked cheerily what I was doing now, there was always the old journalist's fall-back of 'freelancing', although most people know that it means much the same as 'resting' when spoken by an actor, or 'consultancy' from a businessman. Like binning the rejection letters, it was just a sort of sticking-plaster for my self-esteem – and maybe my great idea had its origin in some sort of Zen-like mystical experience brought on by the gently repetitive motion of tossing those screwed-up little balls of crumpled misery across the room. Wherever it came from, it seemed like a way of filling a lot of the gap that the lack of a 'proper job' had left.

## MR NICE?

There was one fairly obvious flaw in my new strategy, which I'll come to later. But in terms of giving me something useful to do, throwing up challenges which would stretch me in all sorts of new directions, and providing a real, urgent reason for getting out of the house, it beat any of the jobs I had seen advertised. It's so simple that I'm almost ashamed to write it down: I started doing a bit of part-time work for a charity – and that is a sentence I never thought I'd write.

I don't think I was particularly unusual in my old life, when the word 'charity' meant little more than the occasional few coins in a collection box, or sending off a quid or two when one of the television appeals hit a tender spot. Anything more than that had a whiff of clerical collars and tree-hugging about it, and didn't really seem to be for me.

And actually, I don't think I had changed that much – an evening a week answering calls for the Samaritans didn't exactly make me a saint. But it did give me a feeling that I wasn't wasting my time, or not all of it anyway, and it gave a lot back to me as well. Why I opted for the Samaritans doesn't matter – there's a huge variety of organisations to choose from. Most people think first of the big international ones like Oxfam or Save the Children, but over 80 per cent of charities in England have incomes of less than £12,000 a year. There's plenty of opportunity there to put the skills you already have to good use, while developing new ones at the same time.

It's certainly not a soft option – not just a way to stop you feeling depressed. There are just as many positive decisions to make about volunteering as there are in a conventional commercial career. And I found out pretty quickly from personal experience that people give you just as much of a scowl if you turn up late whether you're being paid to be there or not. The not-for-profit sector, as it likes to call itself in management-speak, looks for just as professional an approach as a company would.

But in return, you can expect to find significant benefits as well. I'd been working at the Samaritans for several weeks before I found that one of my co-volunteers, who I'd always got on pretty well with, had his own history of redundancy and looking for jobs. It had just happened again for him, and we were sitting in the pub commiserating with each other. 'Being part of the Samaritans was important for me,' he said. 'It gave me a feeling that, even if I didn't have a job, I was doing something useful – making a difference.'

But quite apart from that warm glow of feeling like Mr Nice – quite unaccustomed for me, by the way, and certainly not something to sniff at – there are definite benefits to getting involved 'You have to plan your volunteering just as carefully as you might plan your career,' as one management college academic explained to me. It's worth thinking carefully about what sort of organisation you are going to join – considering the size of it, for instance, and how that affects what you can do for them, and what they can do for you. You don't have to be some sort of latter-day Lady Bountiful or would-be saint: there's plenty in it for you too.

'Charities are a very fast-moving environment, so you can achieve a lot very quickly,' my academic friend said. 'Because there are huge skill gaps, you can find opportunities to prove your practical ability in directions that may not be available in the commercial world. Then the achievements and the abilities you've demonstrated in your charitable work will be reflected in your CV in a way that might give you that vital edge over other candidates for jobs.'

## NEW SKILLS

Put that way, it all sounds a bit cold-blooded and calculating, and rather takes the shine off the new image – still not Mr Nasty, perhaps, but definitely Mr Not-So-Nice-After-All. But there is more to volunteering than simply polishing up your CV – you might simply start to enjoy what you're doing. In the training for the Samaritans, I found myself picking up new skills that I had never dreamed of before – listening to people in different ways, working out how I could help them over the phone, and trying to keep my own feelings in the background. I'm not sure whether skills like that would ever transfer into the commercial world, and I'm not sure that I care, but I do know how much I enjoyed the feeling of learning something that seemed worthwhile.

Several people told me the same thing. 'My father was made redundant as a senior manager in his late fifties, and volunteered to work for his local blind club,' said one. 'From that, he developed a career in local fundraising for them. They benefited from his skills, and he found a new career with a slower pace of life, but a lot of satisfaction. He wasn't earning as much as he had done, but it was an ideal move for him.'

And of course, that's the flaw that I mentioned in my new strategy – never mind not earning quite as much, most volunteers in the not-for-profit sector don't earn anything at all. That's the point, after all. But a lot of people might find that what they get back more than makes up for the lack of money, especially if they can earn a bit here and there in other ways to tide them over. 'One thing I've discovered in the last few years is that I don't need anything like as much money as I thought,' one friend told me. 'I can live pretty frugally, and I'm much more interested in doing something that I enjoy and that I find rewarding.' He was in his fifties and he'd worked out that he didn't have to work again if he didn't want to – 'If I put everything together, I could get by. I wouldn't have as much money as I'd hoped for, but I wouldn't end up living under the arches,' he said. Now he was thinking of taking a spell out of his career and doing some sort of voluntary work with VSO or some similar organisation.

'I want the sense that I'm making a difference, that I have some sort of contribution to offer,' he said. 'I don't want to go somewhere and teach English as a foreign language, because there will be people around who can do that better than I could – but I want to use the skills and capabilities that I have.'

So there are plenty of potential benefits involved in working for a charity – and even if you don't go the whole hog and commit your life to it, there are still lessons to be learned. In my case, I started to learn a bit about competitiveness. I used to be the sort of person who was desperate to win even if I was just racing against my own children in the swimming pool, but learning how to respond to callers to the Samaritans changed all that. It's not a matter of doing it better than anyone else, I discovered – everyone was simply trying to do the best they could, and we all ended up doing it in different ways.

Perhaps that might not go down too well in a business environment, though I think that even there, there may be something to be said for co-operation rather than cutthroat competition. There may be those who suggest, cruelly, that it was odd that the competitive streak of this man who used to glory in his ability to win swimming races with his young children should have withered just as he had reached the age where those same children could watch him dive into the pool, and then put their feet up, file their nails, text their friends, drink a can of Coke and check their emails – and still get to the other end before him. But I think that was just a coincidence.

## NOTES

— Working for a charity may not pay any
money — but it offers you as much as it
offers them.

— Think of small, local charities as well as the
big, famous ones. You may both get more out
of the deal.

— The new skills you pick up may transfer into
a business environment.

# Chapter Thirteen

## So What *Did* I Want?

**B**y now, I had been out of work for more than a year. The money I had been given when I left had been used up so long ago I had forgotten I'd ever had it; I had started freelancing as a journalist for a few magazines in a desultory, unplanned sort of way; and although my saintly other half was showing no signs of resenting the fact that she was picking up almost all the monthly bills, I was feeling increasingly restless and uneasy at my failure to put cash into the monthly pot. It had been bad enough turning into a man who meandered into work like a zombie every morning just because he always had done – it was beginning to feel even worse not meandering into work at all. I did not like the feeling of being a kept man.

It seemed as if I had been prevaricating for far too long – indulging in the luxury of thinking around the question of what I was going to do as if I were Sherlock Holmes on a three-pipe problem. (In fact, with hindsight, I think I was wrong to feel like that; maybe when you are ill the timetable is driven by forces you can't control, but when a relationship is breaking down, or you lose your job, you need to take time to take everything on board. Yes, it's important not to let things drift, but it's also important not to rush at a solution. 'Something must be done; this is something, therefore this must be done' is a piece of false logic that leads many people to torture themselves and leap desperately at the wrong answer. I needed the months I had spent: it was important now to listen honestly to what my mind and body were telling me – and those feelings of restlessness and uneasiness were telling me it was time to change gear.)

I had heard too many stories about people stuck in the wrong job: what was it about their jobs that made some people happy and satisfied? How had they got it right?

## GETTING IT WRONG – AND GETTING IT RIGHT

I once had a friend (the reason for the past tense becomes clear during the story – and it was *very* past tense) who was a big-deal, high-earning, top-of-the-pile accountant. He habitually spent more on lunch than most people spend on a suit of clothes, and enough on a suit to pay for a small family car. ('Whatever *that* might be,' he could have said, as he slipped behind the wheel of his Ferrari – but now I'm starting to embellish the story unnecessarily.) The pleasure he took in all these things, I suspect, was at least equalled by the pleasure he took in describing them to other people – particularly, it often seemed, me. Anyway, one day, having heard for the fifth time about some unbelievably bling piece of spending which also had the near-magical ability to turn itself into a good investment that had stuffed even more cash into his straining coffers, I finally snapped.

'Listen,' I said (rather unnecessarily, since I was talking so loudly that he had no choice) 'even when you have driven your Ferrari up to your massive country house, eaten your eight course dinner, taken off your Savile Row suit and climbed into the bed you have just been telling me about that cost £10,000, you will still never be any more than just one more expletive – deleted accountant.'

Pathetic. Unforgivably rude. And yes, it did show that deep down (well, actually, not that deep down) I was actually jealous. So I should be ashamed of myself – but just for a few minutes, I really enjoyed saying it. And in a way it worked, because we never had the conversation again. More importantly, though, behind that little bit of self-serving bad temper there hid a truth which I do believe is crucially important. We need – or most of us need, because I think my friend in the Ferrari might have been an exception – to do something that we find fulfilling.

The good news about that is that there is an unbelievably wide range of fulfilling ways to make a living. (And yes, I realise that my friend may have found exactly such a thing in accountancy, and I quite understand when you tell me that it was stupid and arrogant of me to believe otherwise. It's just that if you knew him, you wouldn't think so either.) But the bad news is that depressingly few of us manage to find them. Is there anything more soul-destroying than sitting next to someone who wants to tell you how tedious and unrewarding his job is?

Well, yes there is – it is finding that, without ever noticing it happen, *you* have turned into that person. By the time we reach our forties or fifties, many of us have reached the peak of our careers, and we can't hide any more behind the reassuring pretence that a few more promotions, one or two more rungs on the ladder, will lift us into that promised land where we spend our days doing interesting, exciting things that everyone else will appreciate.

So it's little wonder that as we progress through the next few years, many of us develop an unhealthy knowledge of exactly how long we have to go until we retire. We sit in the train and dream of the things we would do if only – until we find that we have become part of the calculator generation, working out desperately what our pensions will be, how much extra we might make if we work a few more years, and what difference a redundancy package might make.

It's a pretty bleak prospect – and if that middle-aged dejection affects so many people, then perhaps it's unavoidable. Except that it isn't. I've also spoken to people who remain as excited about their jobs as they were when they first started them – and these were the conversations I was concentrating on now.

Some of them, like the judge I met on holiday, have reached senior levels in their professions, and can look back on a career that's been successful in its own right. They probably don't have to flinch when they get a letter from the bank, either. Some, like a young executive I know, are still overwhelmed by the challenge and excitement of what they are doing, and the thrill of gradually doing it better – a feeling that may well carry them happily through into middle age, although at some time I suspect they will still have to decide exactly how much the job itself matters to them. But others, like a nurse and a teacher I spoke to, have hardly moved up the career ladder at all in the last 30 years. By any objective standard, their careers had stalled – and yet they positively bubbled over with enthusiasm as they told me about what they did.

So what was it that they had got right?

First, they felt valued. They had taken seriously the old cliché of a thousand Miss World contestants, and found themselves jobs where they were 'working with people'. It didn't have to be a particularly easy relationship all the time – the judge presumably didn't get a great deal of positive energy from the various shady characters he packed off to prison, and a teacher's relationship with his children is not invariably one of bright smiles and sunny days. As for the nurse – well, I'll come to her in a moment. In many ways, she was the most interesting of all. But they all felt that their jobs were worth doing, and they all had that feeling reflected back to them from the people they worked with. Whether it was the parents of the teacher's pupils, or the people who left the judge's court feeling that justice had been done, they were, to put it at its simplest, appreciated.

The nurse had spent more than ten years working in a geriatric ward, which to me, stupid as I was, seemed an almost impossibly bleak and hopeless place to spend your life. 'But why there?' I asked. 'I can see you might feel you had to do it as a duty for a while – but it's a place where you can't win. All your patients die.' She'd clearly been asked this question before, but she was very patient.

'It's the most rewarding place I've ever worked,' she said simply. 'Yes, everyone dies in the end, but some people die peacefully, even happily. Others are kicking and screaming and struggling – but if you care for them properly, you can help them to accept what is happening to them, and die with some peace and dignity. And you can see when that begins to happen for them: you know that you are making a big difference for them.' So the rewards aren't always obvious to outsiders – but they are no less real for that.

Then there was the challenge of the work. For all three, it had to offer them tests that they could only meet by stretching themselves and their abilities. For the judge, that was partly an intellectual exercise: 'There are some judgements – not necessarily the ones you'd expect – that I look back on privately with some pride,' he said. 'It is about applying the law to individual circumstances, whether it's a high-profile case or one that nobody outside the courtroom will ever hear of. When I feel I've met that challenge, I still get real pleasure from it.' The judge I was talking to didn't work in the divorce courts, but the principle there is much the same. The high-profile cases are the easy ones – whoever really cared, for instance, whether Mrs McCartney got £40 million or £10 million or £2 million? Sharing out millions isn't hard, and it's not really important – neither she nor her ex-husband was ever going to be looking at the 'Pensioners' Specials' in the supermarkets. But those are the cases that you read about – the challenging ones are those where the judge is trying to stretch an inadequate income so that two people and their children can have decent lives.

The teacher's attitude was similar to the judge's – it's the challenges that bring the rewards. 'Every teacher likes teaching bright children. It's always exciting to work with kids who are responsive and alert, and to watch them racing ahead. But I sometimes think that the real reward of this job comes when you are dealing with a child who is simply struggling. Sometimes, just sometimes, you realise that you have explained something in a way that they can really relate to – or, even better, you feel that you have passed on some sort of enthusiasm or passion that will stay with them for ever.'

## THE ANSWER

I had been thinking about those conversations for a couple of days, playing them over in my head, when one day my answer came to me. It was, like all the great discoveries, so obvious that it had been staring me in the face for months – years, in fact. I'd known this long before I'd been made redundant. I didn't realise it, but I'd had the answer even before I had been asked the question.

I wanted to write.

Maybe there was nothing strikingly original about that – middle-aged men want to write novels the way small boys want to play football for England. In its way, it's another version of the mid-life crisis, like buying a big motorcycle or getting a tattoo, but a bit more respectable. Even worse, with my habitual cobra-like decisiveness, I wasn't even sure exactly *what* I wanted to write – just about anything anyone would pay me for, I supposed.

But though it wasn't a very detailed conclusion to have come out of all the head-banging and angst, it was at least something to work with. It ticked both the idealistic and the realistic boxes: it would set me challenges, and I would have to stretch myself to meet them. It was what I really wanted to do, and at the same time, it was a way of using the skills I already had. Cobbling together scripts for the evening television news isn't exactly the same as writing

*War and Peace*, but at least I could spell and punctuate. It was a start. I might not make my fortune as a writer – but if I had decided to be a plumber, I would have had to acquire a whole new set of skills and qualifications. And anyway, after we'd spent a day on the road together, my plumber mate had told me that I would starve if I ever tried to do that for a living.

That, of course, might apply to the writing plan too: I had no way of knowing. But I'd written a couple of books before, sneaking time off from my nine-to-five job, and working away in the evenings and weekends, so I knew I could at least put one word after the other, and keep on doing so until I had a lot of words in a row and a lot of pages in a pile. And there were a few people out in the world who had read what I'd written – one or two who had even bought it. If I added all of them together as a potential audience I reckoned it should come to – oh, I paused, trying to do the arithmetic – probably about twelve. Not exactly Dan Brown or JK Rowling material, perhaps, but more than enough for the fingers of two hands, anyway.

In a way, writing wasn't an answer at all – or at least, if it was, it brought a whole new string of questions bumping along in its wake. For a start, the Society of Authors estimates that half the published authors in Britain earn less than the statutory minimum wage in royalties. From the point of view of earning money, I'd be better off looking after a car-park. And then, instead of looking for a new employer, I'd be looking for an agent and a publisher. But somehow the problems didn't seem as intractable now that I was considering something I really wanted to do.

For a start, the freelancing that I had started looked much more appealing when I saw it as a way to support myself while I wrote the things I really wanted to write. I felt a lot keener about looking for new freelance contracts – and that's what I did. Finding the agent and the publisher took some time – but at least I could send the emails and make the phone calls with more enthusiasm when I really believed in what I was asking them. The really daunting problem – what to write about – wasn't a problem at all, as I'd been nursing an idea for years, letting it doze at the back of my mind. I would write about language, about accents and the way we talk, and what they say about us. Yes, there would be a lot of work in doing the research and turning myself into someone who would have something worthwhile to say about it – but work isn't really work when you're enjoying yourself. And I knew that I would.

There were a lot of down times on the way, of course – times when the freelance income didn't add up, times when what had seemed so bright and sparky when I wrote it the night before suddenly had all the appeal of a sock full of wet porridge when I read it the morning after, times when the whole thing just seemed like an interminable slog – but then came that amazing day when the postman brought me a large padded envelope from the publisher, full of page proofs for me to pick over.

And then, of course, there was the day it was published. *A Plum in Your Mouth – Why The Way We Talk Speaks Volumes About Us*. It wasn't my first book, but it was the first one that I had written without the comfort of a regular income – and at last I felt like a real author. And I had found the answer to my question.

## NOTES

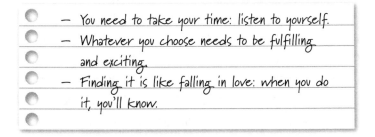

— You need to take your time: listen to yourself.
— Whatever you choose needs to be fulfilling and exciting.
— Finding it is like falling in love: when you do it, you'll know.

# Chapter Fourteen

## Making It Happen

**W**hen you're talking about looking for a new job, it's easy to get bogged down in the practicalities of outplacement agencies, career prospects, interview techniques, and the best way to draw up a CV. But this is a chapter about dreams – although, just in case that seems a bit sentimental, it might be best to start with a nightmare.

When I look back on it now, that's the way it seems – almost like one of those nightmares where you are naked astride a bicycle, pedalling like mad to reach an examination room which seems inexplicably to keep drifting further and further away. You have forgotten everything you ever knew, but for some reason you are desperate to get to the exam . . . You know the sort of thing. Well, this memory may not be quite as bad as that, but it really happened. I was sitting – fully clothed, thank God – in front of a roomful of people who were watching me intently as I slumped, half asleep and apparently incapable of movement, in my chair.

A young woman was bending over me, and urging me to raise my right hand in the air, and all I could think was that, if only I could be bothered, raising my *left* hand would really make her look foolish and give everyone a laugh. But it was all too much effort, and slowly, unwillingly, I raised my right hand simply because it was easier to do as she asked.

I'm not sure that this was what my friends meant when they said I should take a course – any course – but I had signed up for an introductory set of lessons in hypnotism. Some people were there simply out of curiosity, but others clearly had their sights set on a new career in hypnotherapy – helping people stop smoking, curing them of phobias and so on. Maybe a few had unworthy thoughts about how imposing their will on other people might help their sex lives or get them into a high-profile career making drunken slobs do stupid things on stage – but if so, they weren't saying. And I think they would have been disappointed.

I don't think I ever thought seriously about becoming a hypnotherapist, but even so, I got a lot out of the eight days of the course. I learned a bit about hypnosis, I saw real hypnotists at work and tried a little bit myself, and I picked up a few tricks like how to make myself relax. (Breath deeply and count down slowly from, say twenty, always counting on the out breath, if you're interested.) I ended up with a fairly impressive-looking certificate which I will probably put up somewhere if I ever manage to find which drawer I put it in, and a good feeling about myself at what had been a pretty bad time. Best of all, I managed the unexpected trick of impressing my sceptical son: the expression on his face as his hand slowly rose into the air under *my* hypnosis was worth a dozen framed certificates.

## MAKING THEM COME TRUE

But other people got much more out of the course than that: just as I did when I decided that I wanted to write, they got to change their lives. Whether or not the life you imagine for yourself includes your name on the side of a van, a hypnotherapist's brass plate by your front door, or riffling through the first copy of the book that you've written – what it's all about is dreaming.

I don't mean dreaming in the sense of a hypnotic trance, but dreaming in the way that children do when they think of all the possibilities that lie in front of them. It's not something we're supposed to do once we're grown up. It was the Bible that started it: 'Your young men shall dream dreams, and your old men shall see visions,' says the Old Testament. Leave aside the sexism that seems to allow women neither dreams nor visions, however young or old they may be – I don't see why old men should not dream dreams as well. But we still have the same old prejudice – 'Oh, he's just a dreamer' is a fairly damning description of someone who never gets anything done. Dreams are reserved for childhood: when we grow up, we realise that they don't come true, which is why there are so many accountants in the world. There is nothing easier than to think of reasons why we can't possibly do the things we dream of doing.

Later, we may begin to realise that, given a fair wind, our dreams actually may come true after all. For some people, that same hypnotism course which I found so interesting and amusing led into a whole new world. Pamela, for instance, was made redundant from different jobs in accountancy three times during the 1990s. She had been thinking for some time that there were things that interested her a great deal more than accountancy did, and her third redundancy gave her the impetus to do something about it.

'I had been accepting rubbish jobs just to pay the mortgage, and I hated that feeling of being so dependent on being employed by someone else. I'd always been anxious to have financial security, but the redundancies made me think, "Well, what is this so-called security anyway?"' she told me. She did an initial course like I did, and then went on to a diploma course that would qualify her to work as a hypnotherapist. 'I was in my late forties at the time, and it was a second chance in my life to get a more fulfilling career. It just opened the flood gates for me,' she said. 'I had talked about being a doctor when I was a little girl, and my mother had told me not to be silly. Little boys became doctors, she said, and little girls became nurses. I had never thought about it much – but it's odd that I should have ended up in a healing profession like this one.'

Her training was interrupted when she was diagnosed with cancer, but that just made her more determined. 'It confirmed my decision to break away. I'd said in the past that I would do something different one day, and when I was in hospital, I thought to myself, "When is that one day going to come, if not now?"' she said. Now, ten years later, she lives in Gloucestershire with her own practice offering hypnotherapy, life coaching, and stress management courses, and has no regrets – at least most of the time. 'Sometimes when clients are a bit thin on the ground, I wish I had a regular pay cheque coming in. But then I remember the stress and the strain that I used to have, and I think about the things I can do now that I could never have dreamed of. I live in a lovely part of the country; I can see clients in the early evening and give myself time off during the day if I feel like it. I've got my mind free, and I can make my own decisions.'

Philip was one of dozens of IT specialists who fell out of the Enron tree when the company crashed in 2001. 'Most of my colleagues were scrabbling for other IT jobs, but I had already started studying hypnotherapy, and I was fascinated by it. I decided to see if I could make that into my career,' he said. His interest had been aroused when he was cured of insomnia by a hypnotherapist in his late teens: now he has his own private practice, and also lectures on the subject to medical students at a dozen universities. 'I had spent my life working for someone else, and IT was a very unsatisfying industry to be involved in. Everything was very transient: I had reached my late thirties, which is old in that business anyway, and I wasn't leaving any footprints.

'The way to solve that is to change people's lives. With the work I do now, people come to see me with problems, and I can help them go away without them. It's more fulfilling than I could ever have dreamed of when I was working in IT.'

## A SECOND CHANCE TO GET IT RIGHT

There's nothing unique about hypnotism: different people have different dreams. But for many of them, thinking of the dreams they had when they were younger is simply another stick with which to beat themselves when they are feeling depressed: we tell ourselves sadly, angrily, or bitterly that we are too old, that there is not enough time left, or that we have too many responsibilities. It is just another refinement of the same old process of finding reasons why we can't let our dreams happen – and often, years later, we know exactly what it was that we did wrong all those years earlier.

'I guess I just bottled it,' says Christopher now, 20 years on. 'I was just out of university, and I had a choice between a place at the Guildford School of Drama and a job on a magazine. Maybe it was the idea of a regular salary, maybe it was remembering something Alfred Hitchcock said about all actors being no better than cattle – but whatever the reason was, I just didn't do what I really, deep down, wanted to do.'

He went for the safe choice – the job on the magazine – and over the years, journalism treated him pretty well: at different times he had worked in newspapers, magazines, radio, and television, and at the age of 49, he was earning over £50,000 a year at ITV's Sports Channel. But then the channel closed down, and he was back on the market. He had been keen on acting as a young man, although his working life since had left no room for amateur dramatics – but now, a chance remark to a friend led to a small part in a low-budget independent film. And he was hooked again.

'I started freelancing in journalism when I was made redundant, but I suddenly thought: "I don't want to do this for the rest of my life," – so I went home and told my wife that I was thinking of training to become an actor,' he says. 'Far from pointing out all the disadvantages – like the money, obviously – she simply said, "Well, go for it then".'

Those disadvantages were very real, though – instead of earning a good salary as a journalist, he was visiting banks to negotiate a career development loan, and facing a year's training with little or no income. His wife was working as a teacher, but they had two teenage children to consider. The course he applied for at the London Centre for Theatre Studies was timetabled from Thursday to Sunday so that students have a chance to work and earn some money from Monday to Wednesday – but it cost nearly £12,000. It was a big financial decision.

' I thought, "You've just got to do this – you've been given the chance to do what you always wanted to do,'" he says. 'Of course there are money worries late at night, when you lie in bed and think, "I hope this is going to work" but I don't think there was ever a time when I wished I hadn't done it.'

And has it worked? Well, he's now a contented professional actor, earning less than half what he was as a discontented journalist. He's worked in the London theatre, toured with the RSC, and made a couple of small films. 'If I earn £25,000 in a year, I'm doing very well,' he says. 'But the whole family is involved, and I think we're better off as a family for it. I'm doing what I always dreamed of: sometimes I stand in the wings and I almost have to pinch myself to believe that it's all real.'

## A DREAM YOU'D NEVER DREAMED OF

Or take another Chris, who found himself at 50 with a new career he had never even known existed before. After more than 30 years in the RAF Police, he had to start again after the early death of his wife from cancer. When she was ill, he had left the RAF to care for her and their three teenage children, and when she died, he threw himself into arranging her funeral. 'It was my way of coping,' he says now. 'I got the help of an RAF padre I knew, and I organised the funeral as I knew she would have wanted it. I wrote the eulogy, and delivered it myself. It was obviously not easy, particularly with my three children sitting in the front row, but it gave me a real feeling of satisfaction at an incredibly painful time.'

After the service, the funeral director asked him whether he had ever thought of arranging funerals professionally, and put him in touch with the Institute of Civil Funerals. 'I had never heard of it before,' he said. 'It organises be-spoke funerals, with the different elements of the ceremony decided by the bereaved family, filling the gap between the religious services that many people feel uneasy with, and the humanist ones that can seem very unsatisfying.'

So Chris invested time and money in a course that qual-ified him to become a civil funeral celebrant – one of only about 70 or 80 full-time practitioners in the country. 'I do about three or four funerals a week, which is about as many as I could manage, since I need to spend time with the families,' he says. 'Some people need religion when they lose someone close to them, but it can be hard for others to stomach it at that particular time. I think I can understand and empathise with them because I know how I felt when my wife died. I sit with them, and work out how they want to say goodbye in the ceremony. If they want a bit of religion in it, they can have that – it is all entirely up to them.'

For the families, it offers a way of devising a personal tribute that chimes in with the way that they feel – and for Chris, it has provided a career that gives him a real sense of achievement. 'With my RAF pension, it gives me an income that I can live comfortably on – and it means I have a really fulfilling job, helping people get through difficult times. When people say thank you to me after the service, I know they really mean it. I had some interesting times in the RAF, and I thought it would be difficult to beat them. But this job has opened a whole new world to me.'

The dreams that people decide to chase aren't always about making a living. After all, if you don't panic, losing your job may be the first time in your life that you have vistas of free time stretching in front of you; if you are lucky, you may also have more money sitting in your bank account from your redundancy payment than you have ever had before. (If you haven't, those words may be painful to read – but on the other hand, neither have I, and believe me, they were even more painful to write.) But for those who can make the mental leap to see those weeks or months without a job as an opportunity rather than a threat, then there are other dreams that might come true as well.

One woman I have spoken to set off to travel around Europe in a camper van after being made redundant in her fifties; another, in what to my middle-aged, middle-class, conventional mind seems like the worst idea since hedgehogs started curling up into balls to fight off motor cars, started out as a professional poker player. Other people have started university courses, set up smallholdings, or started to advertise themselves as portrait painters. Sometimes, with more or less optimism – or, as in the case of the poker player, mind-blowing lack of reality – they hope to make some money out of whatever it is they do, but generally, they are doing it because they have always wanted to. Every half-baked minor celebrity in reality television blethers on about 'living the dream' after they have been to two parties and a premiere – but these people, studying, writing, delivering lambs in the spring sunshine or parking up for the night in the shadow of the Leaning Tower of Pisa, are doing exactly that.

One good friend took early retirement to start a mini-vineyard in the south of England. And I heard about scores more success stories while I was writing the *Aftershock* column. There were people who became gardeners, zoo-keepers, and long-distance lorry drivers; one man found the police could use his IT skills in the hunt for predatory internet paedophiles – 'Satisfying or what?' he asked – while another abandoned a career in local government which had gone stale to start dealing in antique maps. Some jobs had the potential to turn into full-scale second careers, while others were simply a cobbled-together bridge to carry people over the inconvenient years until they could decently retire and start drawing their pensions – I have lost count of the number of bars that have been opened, from Benidorm to Blackpool, and I could stay at a different bed and breakfast every month that has been started up by someone who had either left or been pushed out of some unsatisfying job.

Well, it was good to talk to them, and when I was feeling like Mr Nice all over again, I guess I got a warm glow from thinking how well things had worked out for them. But they weren't for me. Hypnotherapy wasn't a realistic career option for someone who wouldn't be able to say 'Look into my eyes' without smirking. I'm as vain as the next man, but even I can't kid myself that I look like a star of stage and screen, and as for funerals – well, I must admit that funerals had a certain attraction for me at first. I could do that, I thought – certainly better than the vicar I had heard of who occasionally got mixed up towards the end of a long day. Instead of solemnly calling on the Father, the Son, and the Holy Ghost, he would end the service, standing at the graveside, with the words 'Unto the Father, and unto the Son, into the hole he goes.' Or so I was told.

In fact, I thought as my enthusiasm for the idea grew, I could do the job so well that there were several people in my past working life for whom I would be more than happy to do it absolutely free of charge. Given half a chance, I would rattle through the ceremony, and then put on a clown's hat and a red nose and sing comic songs on their graves. I might put up a picnic table and serve cream teas and chocolate éclairs to passers by while telling jokes and funny stories – *that* would teach them to make me redundant! But no, perhaps I would not be suited to the life of a funeral celebrant either. And anyway, I couldn't quite imagine performing the ceremony in a tee-shirt and jeans: I still hadn't quite got over the thrill of watching my sole remaining suit burn to ashes, and thinking that I would never have to wear another one.

None of that mattered any more. I was listening to their stories from a new standpoint now – from the point of view of someone who, at long last, knew what he wanted to do. But the general principles behind what they had done *were* useful: not just that your dreams can come true after all, but *how* they can come true. It might be a bit over-ambitious in your fifties to set about qualifying as a doctor, but you could still end up in a healing profession by looking at various forms of complementary medicine; if hypnotism fascinates you, you can add to your income as a hypnotherapist by teaching medical students. I might not want to be a journalist again, but I could use the skills I'd picked up over the years in a far more fulfilling way, by writing something that wouldn't be lining the cat's tray by the next morning.

The problems that people threw up when they talked about why they couldn't fulfil their dreams seemed to melt away when I talked to people who had done: yes, my pae-dophile – chasing friend was earning a lot less working for the police than he might have been if he had stayed in the world of corporate management, but it didn't seem to worry him. Pam might occasionally miss the security of her regular salary cheque, but she never seemed to consider leaving hypnotherapy and going back to that world. And no-one, clearly, was ever going to prise Christopher out of the theatre and back into the better-paid, more secure, more conventional life of a television journalist.

And if you had no particular dreams to come true, there was no reason why serendipity, happenstance, chance, call it what you will, shouldn't take a hand. Some of the people I had spoken to seemed to have found challenging and rewarding professions that they had never thought of in their lives. Look as far as you can to one side, and then as far as you can to the other, and that is the spectrum of opportunities that is open to you. The only thing that limits it is how far you can see.

## NOTES

- Don't be afraid to dream — and believe in your dreams.
- Think back to the paths you didn't take — could now be the opportunity to see where they lead?
- Think laterally — you may never have heard of the career that you eventually fit into.

# Afterword

I t's unlikely, however generous-spirited you are, that you will have read this far without one slightly uncharitable question occurring to you: Why should I believe any of this stuff? After all, if this book had been written by Richard Branson to tell you how you could make millions of pounds in business, there would be a certain track record behind it to encourage you to have faith in what it says; Stephen King's book, *On Writing*, comes with the persuasive force of several million novels sold around the world; Andrew Flintoff has a claim to be believed when he talks about cricket, as long as you aren't Australian. But me? About how to get a job? That's a bit like Tim Henman selling you his strategy to win Wimbledon.

There are several answers. First, and most obviously, if this book is about anything at all, it is about the fact that dealing with redundancy is not necessarily the same thing as getting a job. There are as many plans, ideas, and dreams out there as there are people to dream them; some will involve getting back on somebody's payroll, and others will not. The book is about becoming aware of the possibilities that exist, and developing the confidence to make them happen.

More importantly, though, the book doesn't pretend to tell you how to do that. It can't – nobody can. What it can do is to describe how the process of being made redundant, working through it, and coming out on the other side has worked for me, and also – because I've been lucky enough to be in touch through the *Aftershock* column with a lot of other people in similar positions – how it has worked for them.

But what I have at least *begun* to do, I think, over the last few months, is answer the question which I said was at the heart of everything. What do I want? I don't particularly want to be rich – I've seen too many gloomy-faced millionaires to fall for that one. It would be nice to be successful, and have people think how clever I am, but I don't think I'm too bothered about that either. In my mid-fifties, after all, I should have worked out by now how clever I am and how clever I'm not, and what other people think shouldn't matter that much any more. But I would like to be able to say something to my grandchildren and great-grandchildren – to people I care about, who may not be born by the time I die.

One way to do that is by writing books – or rather, since everyone has their own answers to these questions, the way I think *I* might be able do that is by writing books. I don't mean that in any grandiose Tolstoy or Dickens sense – they have spoken to generations all over the world already, and will do so for centuries. Maybe JK Rowling will do the same – so, God help us, may Jeffrey Archer. I don't expect for a moment that the books I write will be read by as many people as theirs – but *A Plum in Your Mouth* has come out, and some people have bought it. I don't care that it's not a best-seller, but I do care that it is going to be one of a number of books that I will write over the next few years. This, at last, is what I want to do – and if I can imagine that sometime in the future, some putative great-grandson of mine might pick one of them up to show to his daughter, and she might think something in it is funny, or interesting, I think that will do for me.

That's my answer, anyway: other people will have their own. In a sense, it doesn't much matter what it is, only that there should be one. And I do know for certain that there isn't a competition to be won.

There are no winners or losers in this particular game of working out what to do with your life. Like many of the best lessons that you learn, this one came – although he doesn't know it – from one of my children. When I was young and stupid, I got a huge amount of enjoyment from playing rugby. There was no better way of spending a Saturday afternoon than knocking people down for 80 minutes or so, being knocked down a few times in return, and then having a drink – as long, of course, as I'd been on the winning side. (Well, I *was* very young.) I grew up, and watched my son doing the same thing – and he loved it too. But then, I watched him swimming, cycling, and running his way through a triathlon, and I realised that the real battle wasn't against the other competitors, but against himself. Finishing the race in a faster time than he had set himself was what counted: you didn't need to beat someone else to win.

It wasn't long after I had started working for the Samaritans, which had probably put the thought in my head that there was more to life than getting in front of the opposition – but it was a revelation to me. I once knew a man who was an insatiable competitor. Whatever he did, he had to be best at; if he blew his nose, he would want you to know that he had blown it better than you could ever have blown yours. He had all sorts of gritty, aggressive little phrases like 'First is somewhere, second is nowhere,' or 'Second place is first loser'. A lot of people in their twenties and thirties are like him – snarling Roy Keanes of the workplace. In fact, industry and commerce are built around them, and if I'm honest, the more carefully I think about how well I knew that man, I seem to remember that I actually *was* him.

Coming first was all that mattered in those days, and it still is to some people. Clive Woodward, returning home with the England rugby team and the World Cup in 2003, even wrote a book called *Winning*, although it was noticeable that when he left New Zealand a few years later, with his British Lions team having been roundly beaten by the All Blacks, he resisted the opportunity to write the obvious sequel. Maybe *Getting Thrashed and Humiliated* would have found a certain readership, but probably not the one he would have hoped for.

Back there in the boxing ring that was corporate employment, every day was a competition. Your success was my failure, and it hurt. For a while, it seemed like a good and productive way to live, but that was a long time ago. In the end, 'dog eat dog' is only a satisfactory philosophy if you are happy to have dog-meat for dinner every day. Now, the best thing I can think of to say about it is that if you're lucky, and possibly with the help of being kicked off the treadmill at some time in your life, you do grow out of that particular frame of mind. Success stories from other people are a reassurance, not a challenge.

And there are a lot of success stories about: the man who urged me, soon after I got the fax that started it all, to take my predicament more seriously was dead wrong. 'For God's sake, this isn't an opportunity, it's a disaster!' he told me. Well, I should have more disasters like this to enjoy – and so should lots of other people. For every despairing or bitter letter or email that comes in to the *Aftershock* column, there are ten people who write to say that redundancy had been the best thing that could have happened to them. Some have ended up back in employment, some have started to work for themselves, and some have simply down-sized, changed their priorities, and slowed their lives down. For some of them, it all happened very quickly, and for others the process took several years – but it *did* happen.

So this book has a few suggestions, but no answers. It's a story, not a textbook. Everything in it comes down to those four crucial words, the question that only you can answer: What do you want?